Amare

A True Italian Love Story

Amare

A True Italian Love Story

SHEILA WRIGHT

iUniverse, Inc.
New York   Bloomington

Amare
A True Italian Love Story

iUniverse books may be ordered through booksellers or by contacting:

iUniverse
1663 Liberty Drive
Bloomington, IN 47403
www.iuniverse.com
1-800-Authors (1-800-288-4677)

Because of the dynamic nature of the Internet, any Web addresses or links
contained in this book may have changed since publication and may no longer be
valid. The views expressed in this work are solely those of the author and do not
necessarily reflect the views of the publisher, and the publisher hereby disclaims
any responsibility for them.

ISBN: 978-1-4401-4172-0 (pbk)
ISBN: 978-1-4401-4166-9 (hc)
ISBN: 978-1-4401-4173-7 (ebk)

Printed in the United States of America

iUniverse rev. date: 6/4/2009

To Morgan and Dylan

In memory of Adamo Gargiulo

This story is true to my memory. Some of the names have been changed to protect privacy.

Prologue

When I first arrive in Sorrento, I have many dreams. Most of them are waking orchestrated ones of making enough money to finance the next leg of my round-the-world trip to Australia. Maybe to Malta where I heard there are lots of private English schools willing to hire under the table.

Two dreams are different, however, occurring in the magical depths of sleep. In the first, I explore an ancient place built into the rocks by the sea. Roman arches shine white in the sun, and turquoise waves splash silver mist over the ruins. My skin feels damp and fresh. A vibration of familiarity surrounds me, as though I have finally arrived at the place where I was meant to be.

The second dream is of a man. He lies beside me on a bed in a large, high-ceilinged room. It is dusk or maybe early morning. I can see the outline of his face in the penumbra, angular with dark hair and eyes. His body is veiled under the sheet. We look at each other, but no words are spoken. It is through his eyes that I perceive the depth of his passion. He looks at me the way I have always wanted to be looked at: with desire, honesty, and unconditional love.

The intensity of the dreams fades, but the feeling remains

seated in the back of my consciousness and I rest my mind on it from time to time. The only word I can find for this feeling is *knowing*—which is different from knowledge since it comes from the spirit rather than the mind. I *know* that no matter what I do and no matter what happens in this life or others, love will be the quiet foundation of my days.

Part One

Chapter 1

At Capo di Sorrento, I leap from the orange *Circumvesuviana* bus and dash through olive groves down the cobbled path to the sea. Old Adamo is waiting. I can see him waving from the sea-spattered rocks below. I carefully negotiate the wooden staircase that leads to our cove and greet him with the obligatory three kisses: left cheek, right cheek, then left again.

"*Porca miseria!*" he cries. "Where have you been? I was so worried!"

In fact, I am only a few minutes late, but this is Adamo. Although I am twenty-eight, he treats me like a young grand-daughter, and I love it.

"Have some freshly roasted chestnuts, *bella*." Adamo speaks in thick dialect. I understand, mainly because he is holding out a large paper bag full of warm nuts, but also because Adamo and I communicate on a deeper level. My grandfathers died long before my birth; I have chosen Adamo and he has chosen me. Sometimes I hardly finish a thought in my faltering Italian and he has already understood. We are from different worlds, different generations, yet our spirits are connected and have come together in this place of my dream.

Right now we are perched on a bench-shaped rock a few feet

above the Mediterranean's gently lapping waves, our backdrop the ruins of Villa Pollio Felice. The shining columns from my dream have long since been washed into the sea. All that remains are a few arches built into the rocky outcrop behind us. The arches, once part of a palace, now support a grassy plateau that commands a view of Sorrento in one direction and the island of Ischia in the other.

The remains of Bagni della Regina Giovanna, Queen Giovanna's baths, are found behind this outcrop, where an archway, part natural, part man-made, allows the sea to flow into a deep hollow the size of a large swimming pool. A tiny pebble beach awaits those willing to climb down the ancient stairs to reach it. Pieces of the ruined palace lie just below the surface of the water. Sometimes I float here and imagine its original splendour.

Every weekday, dodging motor scooters and dog *merda*, I make my way to the Royal School, which, despite the pretentious name, is really a converted apartment where I teach English illegally. With no work permit, I live in fear that the labour inspector will show up and report me to the police; but when I arrive at Capo di Sorrento, all worries lift from my shoulders.

"*Cielo*," says Adamo, pointing with knotted olive-branch fingers to the cloudless sky.

Haltingly, I repeat the word. Adamo's eyes, nestled in sunworn crinkles and blue as the sea, laugh at me. I study Italian in my room at night. Poring over books and newspapers, I memorize verb tenses and words like *smottamento*, mudslide, and *traboccare*, overflow, just because I like the way they sound. But it is here with Adamo that I learn the essentials: *amare, sognare, ridere:* to love, to dream, to laugh. He introduces me to his wife, children, and grandchildren, who welcome me into their home for many languorous lunches. I come away with pearls of old-school Italian wisdom: have children early, live off the land and the sea, keep the family close.

Of course, I understand few of the words that are spoken and often the whole family speaks at once, but somehow, through instinct, sign language, and guesswork, communication happens. Misunderstandings occur, however. Once, while discussing family values, the general opinion seemed to be that it is women's work to raise children.

"But a child needs to spend time with his or her father," I said. My pronunciation of *papà*, father, accent on the last syllable, came out as *papa*, pope, accent on the first syllable.

"*Sì, sì,*" agreed Adamo's wife, indicating a portrait of Padre Pio. "Such influences are imperative in a child's upbringing."

I tried to clear up the confusion, but the conversation had already veered off in another noisy direction. Across the table, Adamo smiled and shrugged. "Have some more wine?" he asked silently, the carafe raised in question.

Every Saturday, Adamo must leave our cove early in order to prepare for *la messa* at the small chapel up the hill. This means he has Sunday mornings free for the usual schedule of chores around his lemon and olive farm and a swim before lunch.

Adamo is reluctant to leave me alone. Although I've been here for over a month, he feels he has to remind me of the dangers that await solo foreign females. "*Stai attenta,*" he warns. "Keep your eyes open. There are *pappagalli* around."

Although the word *pappagalli* means "parrots," in this case he is referring to Italian men (often astride motor scooters) who follow women (usually blonde with walking shoes and a day pack). "*Tedesca? Tedesca?*" they ask, assuming I am German. When I remain silent, walking determinedly, they try all the English phrases they have learned by heart: "Where are you from? You go to beach? You want company?"

I am accosted like this repeatedly in town. A quick *No, grazie*, no eye contact, and a detour into a shop or church is the best bet. Alone at the cove, however, I am a sitting duck. The following scenario unfolds: Adamo leaves. I watch the hydrofoils crossing to Capri and listen to their wake crash against my rock. Then I sense a presence just behind me. It moves closer to my left or right and sits down at a distance that says, "I'm in your space; you have to notice me." After a period of about thirty seconds, the intruder speaks, whether eye contact has been made or not: "Where are you from?" I am left with two options: chat for a while to practise my Italian, or move away and hope not to be followed.

At the Royal School, however, *pappagalli* are my most polite, attentive students. They respect me as the authority on what they most want to learn: English Grammar for the Seduction of Foreign Women. I take advantage of my position to bring them up to date on the workings of the female mind. I explain that in North America, a woman who is followed relentlessly and badgered by incessant questions, grammatically correct or not, is unlikely to warm to the perpetrator. I, in turn, find out that although a southern Italian expects an initial negative response, he believes that persistence is the key. The fact that he rarely gives up easily must be an indication of some rate of success.

There is an Italian comedy sketch in which a man approaches a woman alone on the beach. He asks her if she would like some company. When she answers "yes," he doesn't know what to do.

Today I hear the glad lilt of native English. Two Welsh women introduce themselves and invite me to swim out to the large flat rock that lies in the middle of the cove. "A friendly young Italian man escorted us here from the station," they tell me.

Oh really, I think. So not even women of my mother's generation are exempt from the attentions of *pappagalli*.

"We had no idea how to get here, and he offered to walk with us." They indicate a tall, slim, athletic-looking man who stands on the shore watching something in the direction of Capri. He looks familiar, and I wonder if I've seen him here before.

I spend a little longer with the Welsh women, showing them how to climb on the sharp volcanic rock. Although I could never know this cove the way Adamo does, I am learning where to find soft mossy footholds, smooth crevasses for leverage, and how to walk carefully on the spiny surface to a safe diving place.

Later, we retire to our respective towels to bask in the afternoon sun. From where I sit, I can see the Welsh women and their friend, but they are too far away for me to hear what they are saying.

There aren't many tourists today. It's November, after all, and *la stagione*, the summer season, is long finished. I enjoy the silence and solitude, munching on the chestnuts and sipping the wine Adamo left me. A light breeze brings the pungent scent of rosemary from across the cove. I inhale deeply, appreciating these autumnal blessings with my whole being.

I can't believe it's true, but I have begun a love affair with my old enemy, November. We frolic in the Mediterranean together, forgetting the sordid past we shared in Canada. I gain an absurd sense of satisfaction from knowing that, back home, the skies have turned grey and the first slushy snow has begun to fall along with the last brown leaves.

Footsteps tread on the rock behind me, and my body tenses. A man, hardly more than a teenager, stands beside me, so close I can smell the lingering odour of cigarettes on his clothes. "May I sit here?" he asks, with a leering grin.

"I'd rather be alone," I reply, certain I am wasting my breath. Sure enough, he sits down, practically on my towel. I get up and start to collect my things. Before I have a chance to devise my next plan of action, I hear my name.

"Sheila! Come and join us!" call the Welsh women. They have been watching and are rescuing me. I wave gratefully and move my things. Their Italian friend greets me. "You must watch for such men," he says.

I start to laugh, since he's certainly no better himself, but stop in mid-thought, mid-smile. There is genuine warmth in his eyes, and I am struck by what seems to be a memory of him. It is there on the tip of my mind, but I can't place it. I am so convinced that I must know him from somewhere that I break my ask-no-questions-of-strange-men rule and come right out with it: "Have you been here before?"

He looks at me for a moment before answering, and I feel he is searching for something, perhaps the right English words.

"Not this year," he says slowly, choosing each syllable. "I am from Napoli. Is some distance."

At this, my rational mind shoves the memory back, away from the place where I can almost grasp it. I have never been to Naples. I can't possibly know him.

The Welsh women start to pack up. "Good-bye Sheila, good-bye Gino. We must be off. Thank you both for a lovely day." They leave, and I am left alone with the Italian man.

"I am Gino," he says. "Is pleasure to know you, Sheila."

Gino has a mauve and turquoise day pack into which he slides the book he had been reading.

"What's that?" I ask, breaking my rule again. He hands me a slim pink and grey paperback, taller and wider than most, with a small red heart on the front.

"I buy today," he tells me, "with *intenzione* to read here in this beauty spot."

My Italian is improving daily, but I stumble mentally over the title: *Và dove ti porta il cuore.* Gino translates it for me. His soft, rolling voice fills the words with meaning, and the phrase "follow your heart" sings itself into my soul. A simple phrase, a cliché, but I can't help embracing it. I feel as if I now know something about Gino, something more profound than anyone would expect from a first encounter.

Chapter 2

"What a sin!" Gino exclaims when I tell him I have never been to Naples. On our walk back into town from the cove, he tells me of the *bellezze d'arte* hidden in the churches, castles, palaces, and squares, and just as enticingly, of the restaurant where pizza was first made. "I will be your guide," he says. "If you agree, I meet you ten o'clock tomorrow morning at Stazione Centrale."

I agree.

My landlady, Mamma Russo, does not. "Those *napoletani* are nothing but trouble!" she shouts across the breakfast table, gesturing wildly with her *biscotto*. "If you even *think* of leaving here, I'll lock you in your room!" She knows there is no lock on my door, but she is making a point in her usual fiery way. From my tiny apartment at the end of the hall, I often hear her bellowing at her three children. Now I feel like one of the teenagers—irritated by her overbearing caring.

I hope that Gino will show me the good side of Naples, the one bursting with vitality and tradition, where pizza chefs sing "*Funiculi, Funicula*" while slinging powdered dough in the air. But Mamma Russo's words feed my doubt and apprehension. I've heard the rumours about Naples, that it is a city of thieves and tricksters, mobsters, and money launderers.

My guidebook warns of *scippatori* on motor scooters who snatch jewellery and handbags as they tear past. It tells of hypodermic needles strewn around the train station and describes the *trucchi* played on unsuspecting tourists who purchase a video camera only to find later in their hotel room that the box contains nothing but a brick.

When I arrived in Naples by train in September, I didn't even step outside the station. Instead, I immediately boarded the *Circumvesuviana* train bound for the Sorrentine Peninsula, thirty miles away. I passed through the grimy periphery of the city and through countless squalid drug-lord-ridden suburbs built in the shadow of Mount Vesuvius.

Tunnel after mountain tunnel, the air became fresher and the houses less dilapidated until finally I burst into a world of orange groves, rocky beaches, tufo cliffs, and aquamarine sea. I looked across the bay to see that I had come a semicircle away from Naples; there it was, barely visible in the distance, harmless.

Now, every evening, I sit by my window in my room atop Colli di Fontanelle and watch the infamous city twinkle and glitter like a peaceful village far across the water. I wonder about its secrets, its history, the families it holds.

I can't bear to listen to Mamma Russo's rantings, so I lie. "Didn't I mention that Gino is a friend of Adamo's family? You know, the people who feed me lunch on Sundays." I throw in the food part so that she will recognize them as fellow protectors-of-young-travellers. She has taken me under her wing and although it's not included in the rent, provides me with breakfast every day and often leaves a plate of dinner for me to find when I get home from work.

I consider including something about Padre Pio, just for good measure, but she relents. Minutes later I dash out the door with a quick "*ci vediamo dopo,* see you later," before she can start again.

I wait for the bus in the square. It's late as usual. Uncertainty threatens to overthrow my enthusiasm, so I concentrate on the view, peering down the mountainside over the tops of olive and orange trees that hide fragrant wild herbs like rosemary, chicory, and borage. My gaze travels out to sea and across the bay to Naples, but before doubt has a chance to take hold in my mind, the minibus whines to a halt in front of me.

I bid *buongiorno* to Pasquale, the driver. The other passengers watch me. I am *la canadese*, the only foreigner in Colli di Fontanelle, unless you count Salvatore *o'canadese*, who once lived for a few years in Montreal and now owns a restaurant farther up the mountain.

Outside the window I see the one-eyed shepherd with his mob of mangy, disobedient sheep. They squeeze in front of the bus, occupying the whole road in a stumbling mass of wool and hooves. And the road, carved as it is between stone-walled terraces, is much too narrow to allow the bus to pass. I am nervous and agitated, coffee and milk curdling in my gut as we creep behind the flock like a giant orange wolf.

By the time we reach the train station, I have nervously opened and closed the zipper on my day pack so many times, the woman in front of me has started to mutter and throw evil glances over her shoulder. I run into the station and buy my ticket. I have five minutes to wait, so I pace the platform. Once I'm on the train, there will be no turning back. It would have to be a real emergency for me to get off at any of the towns along the bay. With squalid degradation on one side and Vesuvius, one of the world's active volcanoes, towering over the other, the fifty-minute trip cannot come to an end soon enough.

Hard plastic seats add to my discomfort. It is Sunday, but the train is full. Again I seem to be the only foreigner, and I feel eyes roving over my blonde head, hiking shoes, and bright red pack. I grip my bag tightly when new passengers board at the no-man's-land stations of Torre Del Greco and Leopardi. The station at Pompeii is newly painted terra-cotta and white. I feel disproportionately relieved to see a few tourists get on.

As the train pulls into Naples, I search the platform for Gino.

What if he's not here? I will be impelled without direction, bull-dozed along by the crush of disembarking passengers.

But there he is. Standing tall amongst the crowd, mauve and turquoise pack slung over his shoulder. As I move closer, carried on the rush of bodies, I see him smile, with eyes as well as mouth.

"I thought you not come!" he says. "You were afraid? Perhaps of me, a little?"

"Yes, no … I don't know. I'm just glad to see you!"

He takes my hand, and I am suddenly grounded; he will be my lifeline in this city. Naples is no longer terrifying. I feel only elation and eager anticipation as we walk out of the train station into the square.

We cross Piazza Garibaldi, a huge square full of idling orange buses. I cough, and Gino increases his pace. The square is circled by roaring, fume-sputtering traffic. There are lights, but drivers and pedestrians alike ignore them. One driver slows down at a red light, and the cars behind instantly break out in a frenzy of honking. Gino waits for a pause in the pandemonium, grabs me tightly by the arm, and we fling ourselves to the other side. We catch our breath in a quieter side street, where only the blat and whine of motor scooters prevails.

Gino notices the shock on my face. "Sunday traffic is light. Other days are much worse. Come, I show you good side of Napoli."

Gino positions himself street-side so that I am protected from pickpockets. It has started to drizzle, so we walk arm in arm under his umbrella. We window-shop along Corso Umberto, one of the main commercial streets in Naples, then continue up Via Duomo, past shops filled with wedding gowns, designer shoes, and *bomboniere*, the small gifts given out at weddings. The Duomo is a typically imposing cathedral, with wide steps leading to tall arched doorways. Beggars wait for those who wish to lighten the load of eternal sin.

Inside, Gino explains that the Duomo is dedicated to the patron saint of Naples, San Gennaro. Twice a year, in the presence of hundreds of believers, a priest holds up a vial containing the solidified blood of the saint. Then, before the eyes of everyone, or at least those in the first row since the vial is rather small and the church is rather dark, the blood liquefies. We can't see the blood today; it is locked up with other relics and treasures.

Gino guides me to a small side door near the entrance. Stone steps, hollowed with the imprint of time, lead us down under the cathedral into the cool heart of ancient Neapolis. Descending past Roman ruins, we reach Greek ones at the bottom. I am inside layers of history for the first time in my life. The scent of damp earth and rock imbued with the sweat and blood of three civilizations leaves me dizzy and speechless.

We go next to the excavations under the church of San Lorenzo Maggiore. We walk along a Roman street directly beneath the modern one, a street that leads us through the market area where shops and restaurants are still visible, having been covered and preserved in a mudslide four hundred years before Pompeii was struck by a similar disaster. Descending further, we find the remains of a Greek temple.

"These are hidden places that many *napoletani* never discover," says Gino. "People are too caught up in the *moderno* world to take the time to appreciate our history."

Gino's effort to speak English delights me. He takes his time, slowly selecting each word and holding eye contact to make sure I have understood.

He remembers a teacher he once had: "We would leave the stuffy classroom and musty old *libri* behind and go out into the *città* to touch the past with our own hands. It was in this way that I came to know the treasures of my *città*."

"You are lucky," I say. "We often take for granted the wonders that are close to us."

The sun has come out, so instead of going to a restaurant for lunch, we stop at an *alimentari*. Gino steps up to the deli counter and orders huge *prosciutto* sandwiches on fresh-baked loaves. He buys a bottle of red wine as well, and the shopkeeper loosens the cork and offers us two plastic glasses. We walk to the waterfront, where we recline on the massive volcanic rocks and devour our meal. Fishing boats, tour boats, hydrofoils, and ferries fill the harbour.

"The sea is traffic-jammed, just like the city," I comment.

"This is *niente* compared to how it used to be. In the seventies, there were so many *motoscafi* bringing contraband cigarettes and so many police boats chasing them, you could never have enjoyed a peaceful *pranzo* in this place."

After lunch we continue our tour of the *centro storico*. In the church of Gesù Nuovo, along with the usual relics of saints, imposing statues, and inlaid marble, is a small dark room full of tiny metal body parts. The older ones are pinned to the wall and under glass; the newer ones hang from silk ribbons on a special altar.

Gino explains that they are offerings of thanks from people who have been healed. "If you pray to *Gesù* and are cured of lung cancer, you give a lung. If you had a brain tumour disappear, you give a brain."

I become at once hyperconscious of all my body parts, feeling the pulse and heat of my inner organs, the stretch of skin over bones and muscle. I stand close to Gino, wondering if he can feel how alive I am.

Across the street in the cloister of Santa Chiara, we rest on benches beside fountains, hanging vines, and columns covered with colourful *maioliche*, ceramic tiles depicting scenes from ancient Naples. Then, on a tiny street just off Piazza San Domenico Maggiore, Gino pays a few lire to a man in a dark booth and we enter the silent Cappella di Sansevero.

In the centre of the chapel lies a marble sculpture of the prostrate, veil-covered body of Christ. The marble 'veil' seems almost transparent, showing the facial features and bone structure below.

"The *Principe* of Sansevero was an alchemist," says Gino.

"*Legenda* states that he was able to preserve human bodies. Many *napoletani*, superstitious by nature, like to believe that this sculpture is actually a man turned to stone by the *Principe*."

I am almost inclined to join the believers when we reach a small room in the basement. There, preserved under glass, we find two skeletons complete with veins and arteries. A short paragraph, written in several languages, explains that these bodies were possibly injected with a hardening fluid while still alive, over three hundred years ago.

Returning to the chapel, I notice a statue of a fisherman in one corner. He has a rope net thrown over one shoulder.

"How interesting to combine rope and marble," I say to Gino.

"Look closer."

I am within arm's reach of the sculpture before I realize the net is marble, too. We stand in silence, admiring the intricacy of the carving, letting the enchantment of the room envelop us.

After this extraordinary tour of cathedrals, churches, and chapels, we take the *funicolare* up to Castel Sant' Elmo where we walk the parapets, viewing the entire city, Vesuvius, and the islands of Capri, Ischia, and Procida, from above. Amazingly, we have the place to ourselves. The distant cacophony floats up to us, but it is the sound of the sea breeze in my hair that I notice most. I lean against a turret, watching the living maze of streets far below. There is only one road that lies straight across the city.

"That is *Spaccanapoli*," says Gino. "It is named like this because it breaks the city in two. *Spaccare* means to break." His face is close to mine as we both peer through the same narrow opening. Gently, he turns me around so that my back is to the city. He lifts his hand to my cheek. "May I kiss you?"

Suddenly dizzy with an acute sense of the empty space tumbling away behind me, I nod.

"Don't worry," he says, pulling me against him. "I won't let you fall."

Then his soft, full lips touch mine. The kiss is all too brief and when we separate, I think I should be afraid, up here alone with a virtual stranger. But there is no room for fear in the haze of contentment that surrounds me.

"There is one last stop to make," says Gino.

"What's that?" I breathe, unable to imagine anything past this moment.

"Dinner at *da Michele*, the birthplace of pizza."

And so we descend into the city, where we hold hands across a table in tiny, crowded *Antica Pizzeria da Michele*. We share a *margherita* pizza made with tomatoes, garlic, basil, and fresh buffalo mozzarella. We share a large *Nastro Azzurro* beer. We share ourselves. Gino tells me about his job in the family glove factory on the other side of the city. I tell him about my plans for Australia. As I speak, I am certain that my path will be filled with adventure. I begin to wonder, however, whether Australia is really where I want to go.

Chapter 3

On Monday morning, I peek inside the door of the Royal School before entering. The administrator, known secretly to staff and students as The Crazy Lady, sits behind her desk, clouds of smoke from her cigarette mingling with mad-scientist hair. No chance of sneaking in unnoticed.

"*Sei in ritardo*," she growls as soon as I set foot in the small lobby.

She's right. I am late. There is a train strike today so I had to walk the two stops from the base of the mountain to Sorrento. "There was a strike," I say.

"*Sciocchezze*! Ridiculous! I arrived from Napoli this morning!"

This is the thing about Italian train strikes. They happen for precise times, say, from 2:30 to 3:15, but before and after, everything runs normally. Only people unfortunate enough to travel within those times have their day thrown out of whack. Unless you read the notice posted at the stations (in this way, the *Ferrovia Italiana* is very considerate), you would never know about the strike.

My students are waiting, so I walk into the classroom and close the door on the glare that follows me.

"The Crazy Lady is angry?" asks Costantino.

I roll my eyes, sit down, and open my book entitled *The Callan Method*. I find the page marker from the day before, turn back six pages, and start reading. "Is this a shoe?" I ask, holding up a pen and pointing to Antonio.

"No, it is not a shoe, but it is a pen," he answers.

"Are there two pens?" I ask the student next to him.

"No, there aren't two pens, but there is one pen."

This exchange is printed word for word in my book and in theirs. We did the same thing last class and the class before. I am required to turn back a certain number of pages each time and although we cover seven or eight pages, only two of them will be new material. REPEAT, REPEAT, REPEAT screams the banner above The Crazy Lady's desk. And this is what we do, at least for the first part of the class. I hurry through the text at lightning speed in order to get to the real stuff. Books remain open, however, in case The Crazy Lady or her husband Julio bursts in.

This is my class of *pappagalli*. Most of them are in their early twenties, waiters and barmen at the innumerable hotels and restaurants in Sorrento. "How were things at work last night?" I ask Costantino.

"Good. Much tips. One man, he take *gli avanzi* to his room. Italian people never take *gli avanzi*. How do you say *gli avanzi*?"

Here lies the challenge for me. It is not necessary to speak Italian in order to teach English. In fact, The Crazy Lady insists that I speak only English and won't even allow English/Italian dictionaries in the class. But sometimes I wish I could come right out with the answer instead of working around it for ten minutes. This can be a useful exercise in itself, however; Costantino must now try to explain the context around his question. I finally deduce that *gli avanzi* means "leftovers." We are both one word richer.

At this point, Julio erupts into the room.

"Sheila, I am taking over. My wife needs to speak with you."

I sense a collective groan from the room. A native of Spain,

Julio speaks with an accent the students find difficult to understand. He is also fiercely dedicated to The Method. The Crazy Lady speaks no English whatsoever and has no interest in learning. I steel myself for the encounter and leave Julio my book, marked at "Is this pen red? No, but it is blue."

Julio settles himself in my chair. "Right, boys, whose turn is it?"

Costantino heaves a sigh and raises his hand.

The Crazy Lady is on the phone, but hangs up as I take a seat in front of her desk.

"*Allora*, Sheila, *c'è un problema.*"

This much I understand. There have been nothing but *problemi* since I started working here. I don't have a work permit. I don't even have a *permesso di soggiorno*, residency permit. This situation is normal; half the English teachers in Italy are working *al nero*, under the table. Julio and The Crazy Lady knew my status from the beginning and still agreed to hire me. For peanuts, of course, and in order to continue paying me less than minimum wage, they constantly remind me of my precarious position.

"*Siccome tu sei clandestina …*" she starts.

Clandestina! Imagine, me, an English teacher from Canada, clandestine, outside the law! This is my new identity, and it's rather exciting. I gather from her raspy smoke-filled rantings that Thomas, an Australian teacher, has been tracked down by the police and has had to leave the country. This shocks me. I hadn't taken the threat of discovery seriously.

The Crazy Lady wants me to file a request for a *permesso di soggiorno* at once. She has been told by her advisors that all I have to do is pretend I'm a tourist, fill out some forms, pay a small fee, and the authorities will stay off my back for at least three months. This would be great. I'm certainly not ready to leave yet.

"*Và dalla polizia!*" she bellows, nicotine-stained finger thrust toward the door.

The police station is a couple of blocks away, behind a high iron fence. I push a button, tell a voice I am a tourist looking for a *permesso di soggiorno*, and the gate swings open. Inside, I wait for half an hour before several forms are produced for me to fill out. I pore over them, trying to remember whether *cognome* means surname or given name and at which town I crossed the Italian border.

Then there is a meeting with the *Maresciallo*, a broad man with a gruff voice, who interrogates me: "Why have you waited so long to apply? Where are you planning to go next? Are you working?"

I tell him what I think he wants to hear, especially on the last one, since only members of the European Economic Community or those with valid work permits are allowed to hold jobs. He seems satisfied. Another officer comes to take my photograph. The forms are signed and stamped and placed in a folder. I pay.

"You will be informed when the *pratica* is complete," says the *Maresciallo*.

I consider reporting back to the school, but decide to wait until tomorrow. Instead, I check my bag to make sure I have my swimsuit and board the bus for Capo. As we lurch through Sorrento's narrow streets and up towards the cape, I wonder at my attraction to this place and why I am prepared to do whatever it takes to stay a little longer.

Even before I met Gino, there was a bond between me and the peninsula. I had even dared to find an apartment before finding a job. How had I been so certain I was meant to be here, that this was the place where I should stop? There are only three tiny English schools on the peninsula, none of them able to offer much pay. And the pay was irrelevant, since none of them had offered me a job. "Perhaps in a few weeks," was the best response I could get.

I didn't notice the hold Sorrento had over me at first. I had booked into the youth hostel with Em, an Australian woman I'd met up north in Cinque Terre. Since Em had only a few days to stay before heading back to Rome, I played tourist with her, visiting Pompeii and Capri, dining on pizza and *gnocchi*, learning the bus route to Positano, a stunning beach town on the Amalfi Coast. We met up with other Aussies who were not afraid to be out there in the world simply for the sake of travel itself.

After Em left, the dreams began. I felt myself loathe to depart and was almost relieved to hear that my contact in Malta didn't encourage a visit during stormy October. Using the infrequent ferry schedule as a further excuse to hang around longer, I began to wonder if Salerno, a university town down the coast, might be a better option. But I never went there.

One day, on the table in the youth hostel common room, I found a map of the coast. Circled in red was a promontory a few miles away. I picked up the map and started walking.

It was a long, hot walk but I was pulled like an iron filing to the magnet of Capo di Sorrento. At the village square, I turned down a steep cobbled path leading through lemon and olive groves to the sea. The slippery cobblestones impelled me forward as I struggled to keep an even pace. The sun glinted off the sparkling sea, blurring my vision, so that, at first, I didn't notice I was standing on Roman ruins. I focused instead on the flat rocks below.

A suntanned, spry old man was there, waving to me, beckoning as though he had been waiting and was glad I had finally arrived. "*Ciao, bella, mi chiamo Adamo,*" he said, gesturing for me to sit beside him. And I did, on that day and many days afterwards.

I moved out of the hostel and up the mountain to Colli di Fontanelle; Sorrento apartments were out of my price range. Knowing the transient nature of language schools and their employees, I felt sure that if I waited long enough, a position would come up. And it did: a teacher quit the Royal School, leaving a gap that needed to be filled immediately. I stepped in, my new roots fortified with purpose.

That was only six weeks ago. But now, as I reach again the cobbled path to Adamo's door and the sea, I wonder if my young roots will one day be entwined with Italy like those of an ancient olive tree.

"*Ciao,* Sheila!" greets Adamo, as he hauls open the solid iron gate. "Come see what we're working on today."

With the heavy clang of the gate closing behind me, the Royal School and the police station fade to other worlds. Adamo's orchard is humming like a hive of worker bees. The whole family has been collecting olives from nets strung under the trees like giant cobwebs. Adamo's son, Mariano, and his grandson, Adamo Jr., are shovelling the olives into a sorter.

"*Vutt' abbascie!*" shouts Adamo, showing me how to encourage the olives down the sorting ramp. "*Vutt' abbascie!*" he says again, demonstrating with exaggerated gestures until I understand that *vutt' abbascie* means "push them down."

I had hoped that Adamo would come swimming with me, but I see he is much too busy. Instead, I help with this simple, repetitive task until Adamo's wife peeks out from the kitchen window, sees me, and calls us for coffee. To her, I am still an honoured guest, one that must be shown respect and plied with sugary espresso every time I show my face. She invites me to stay for dinner, too, but I decline. I don't want to miss the last bus to Colli.

After our rejuvenating espresso shot, we return to the orchard, where I pass an hour or two in happy oblivion under the lemon and olive trees.

"*Vutt' abbascie,*" Adamo says again, asking me to repeat.

"Voot a bash," I stammer, and he laughs.

"You have to put your heart in it, be *apassionata.*"

I try again, hating my accent.

"It's not your fault," he sympathizes. "The English language has no *passione.*"

It isn't just the language. My whole life lacked passion before Italy.

Chapter 4

My *permesso di soggiorno*, when it comes through, will give me three to six months in Italy. Should I even stay that long? Australia is waiting. My work permit will expire if I don't get there within a year. The whole idea was to travel east around the world, make money here and there, and finally arrive in Australia to work for up to a year. England, France, Germany, Italy. That's how far I've come so far. I needed somewhere to heal after France. This seems to be the right place.

France was supposed to be an old friend, an ally in adventure from university days. Instead she turned on me, mocking my boldness. At first she enticed me with her charms, a meeting with an old lover and a tryst with a new one. I was fooled into smug complacency, and it was easy for her to shatter my illusion.

I couldn't resist one more night with my new lover and on impulse, instead of boarding the train for Germany, left my pack in a locker at the Gare du Nord and walked back to his place. I took only my daypack with me. In it were my wallet, passport, camera, toothbrush, a change of underwear, and a ticket to Bonn.

The next morning, I returned to the station to find a gaping hole where my pack used to be. The door to the locker had been pried open. Everything was gone. All the worldly goods I had packed for my trip to Australia plus my life's savings, six thousand dollars in travellers' cheques.

A bored police officer listened to my description with a look that told me I'd never see my belongings again. He wrote the report anyway, heaving a sigh as he momentarily abandoned his *café au lait* and *pain au raisin*. Then he dismissed me with a flick of his pen and a curt *adieu*.

Eyes prickling with impending tears, I found a telephone and dialled the international number for American Express. Ms. Amex didn't believe my story. Who would be stupid enough to leave six thousand dollars in a train station overnight? Actually, she used the word "negligent," but I heard it as "stupid," which is certainly how I felt. She said I would have to call back once they had verified my identity. I gave her all the necessary information and hung up.

I boarded the next train to Bonn and sat staring despondently out the window. My reflection stared back, a dispirited image gliding over the Parisian outskirts. Light rain made teardrops on my transparent face. I couldn't even manage in Paris; how was I supposed to survive in all those unknown places between France and Australia? Even with my six thousand dollars, I would still need to find work along the way if I wanted to explore the world before arriving at my final destination. I had big plans and an Australian work permit. Right now I doubted my ability to complete anything more than this visit to a dear friend in Germany.

In Bonn, I cried on my friend's shoulder. An experienced traveller herself, she moved my mind off the tragedy and back onto the adventure. She even booked me a ride to Florence with a young man named Hans. Three days later, my cheques came through. I went shopping and bought some clothes, shoes, soap, and shampoo. That night I packed my new life into a canvas shopping bag and dreamt of Italy.

Hans dropped me off at the train station. Florence held good memories, and I hoped she wouldn't delude me the way Paris had.

I went inside the station and bought a newspaper full of classified ads called *La Pulce* and a pocket-sized Italian/English dictionary. The English word babysitter jumped out at me from several ads. Also the words *inglese* and *lezioni*, which I knew. I managed to decipher several ads for English teachers or English-speaking live-in babysitters. I bought a phone card and started dialling. "Do you speak English? *Parlez-vous français?*"

All the people I called spoke a little of one language or the other, and I quickly narrowed down my options. Some were too far out of town. Some wanted a full-time sitter, housekeeper, and cook; I hadn't spent ten months obtaining a certificate in Teaching English as a Second Language just to become a servant.

I eliminated all the ads I had circled except one: *Cercasi babysitter madrelingua inglese. Vitto, alloggio e compenso.* Signor Viscardi was a divorced lawyer who spoke perfect French. He was looking for a live-in nanny to look after his six-year-old daughter. She was in school, so my job would be to drop her off, pick her up, and in the evenings provide her with casual exposure to English language and culture. There would be no cooking or housework as there was already an Italian housekeeper. I would have my days free to find other work as a private English teacher. We arranged to meet that evening at his office.

I spent the day wandering around Florence, rediscovering the places I had visited eight years earlier: the market, full of leather and Merino wool, the Ponte Vecchio with its ancient arches and gold merchants, the Duomo, the many squares and parks full of pigeons and old men playing *bocce.* The delectable aroma of steamy cappuccino and fresh-baked *cornetti* greeted my nostrils on one corner, while a cheese stall sent out a pungent assault from another. And from balconies above wafted basil, garlic, and roasted scents like peppers or eggplant *alla brace.* I could be blindfolded and still know Italy by her *odori.* It was just as I remembered, and the added thrill of anticipation surrounded everything with a joyful new allure.

I found a room at the youth hostel, took a shower, had some

bread with *prosciutto* and *provolone* in the common room, then stepped out into the fragrant Florentine evening in search of Signor Viscardi's *studio*.

The thing about old Italian cities (and they are all old) is that the street numbers, when visible, do not necessarily correspond to anything. One building will have an ancient engraved *26* and the next will have a spray-painted *407 A*. Some will have both engraving and spray paint plus a brass plaque with yet another number on it.

It took me a good hour to find Signor Viscardi's office. His secretary took my name. I found a chair and a stack of magazines in the waiting area. After half an hour, a man I imagined to be a client came out and left. Signor Viscardi's voice droned on the phone for another twenty minutes. The secretary started to clear up her things, waved to me, and left. It was eight o'clock.

Had Signor Viscardi forgotten about me? I leafed through yet another magazine and had just congratulated myself on deciphering a whole paragraph with the help of my dictionary when I heard a door open and close. Signor Viscardi darted out, briefcase in hand, straight past me. I nervously choked out a *"buonasera"* and he spun towards me.

"Dio mio!" he exclaimed. "I completely forgot you were here! Come, come, we'll go into my office."

I hurried after him, disturbed by his agitated demeanour. He put down his briefcase and seated himself behind a gargantuan oak desk, immediately regaining his composure and taking on that cool aura of professionalism common to lawyers all over the world.

I let out my breath and tried to relax. I had nothing to show him. My résumé, diplomas, and references were stolen in Paris. "I can easily have new copies sent from Canada," I promised.

He leaned back in his plump leather chair, folded his manicured fingers on the desk, and contemplated me from across the vast expanse of wood. He was Latin-lover handsome, just as I had imagined from his voice on the phone. His gaze roved, lingering brazenly here and there.

"*Don't blush, don't blush,*" I repeated to myself, but an uncomfortable and inevitable heat began to spread through my body. I readjusted my legs, brushed an imaginary strand of hair from my face.

"The most important thing," he began, "is that you should read to my daughter in English, of course, but also in Italian. You don't need to understand the text, just try to pronounce the words correctly. *Vieni*, give it a try, it is really very simple." He motioned for me to come around to his side of the desk, where a hardcover book lay open. "Try to read this."

He pulled me close so that I was perched on the arm of his chair. I had to lean over him slightly to see where he was pointing. I read a sentence and stopped.

"Very good," he murmured. "Now try the next line." He slid his arm around my waist, wrenching me off balance so that I landed in his lap. Startled, I scrambled ungracefully out of the trap that his chair, desk, and arms had become. I stood shaking while his mouth went through the motions of apologizing for "the accident." His eyes, however, wore a hard leer. "Think about the position. I'll expect a call from you …."

I had reached the door of his office before he finished speaking. My fleeing footsteps were loud on the marble floor and stone stairway. There was no one in the street, where it was now dark and raining. I bolted all the way back to the hostel.

Without undressing, I climbed into my bunk. No one else was there. I envied my roommates, out dining and exploring together. Whether from intense loneliness, momentary revulsion, or true gut instinct, I understood that Florence was not the place for me. I had to move on.

The next morning, an American woman told me about her recent trip to Cinque Terre: "Five small villages by the sea, great hiking, terrific youth hostel run by a friendly woman named Mamma Rosa."

I knew where my next stop would be. No looking for jobs, just relaxing by the Mediterranean and walking the hills. The perfect place to contemplate my next move.

At Riomaggiore, Mamma Rosa and her herd of cats were at the train station to greet me and a couple of other travellers. Waves crashed against the rocks below the station, sending welcome sea mist into my lungs. The sun was beginning to set as Mamma Rosa showed me into her large kitchen. Travellers of all nationalities were cooking, eating, talking, playing with the cats.

I deposited my bag in the room she assigned me and dashed off to the corner *alimentari* to buy dinner supplies: penne, fresh tomatoes, basil, garlic. My mouth watered at the thought of a home-cooked meal. Finding a couple of vacant pots in the kitchen, I boiled water for the pasta and started to make a quick sauce with the tomatoes, basil, and garlic.

Mamma Rosa darted over to the stove. "You can't make *salsa* without olive oil and salt!" she scolded. Then she threw a handful of salt and the remainder of a bottle of oil into the pot. "*Ecco*! That's better. But you really should have left the basil until the end. Did you put salt in the pasta water?"

I shook my head, inspiring her to grab another two handfuls of salt from the bucket on the counter. She tossed them into the water, then bustled off to help another hapless cook. I poured the sauce over the penne and dubiously took a mouthful. It was heaven. I ate two helpings and put the rest in the fridge.

I had been too busy with cooking and eating to start a conversation with anyone. Now a young woman smiled at me from across the table. She had that healthy outdoorsy look that immediately inspires confidence.

"I'm Em. This is Tim," she said, indicating the young man next to her. "We're from Australia. We were just going down to the harbour to see how it's illuminated at night. Do you want to come?"

I went, and we became instant friends. They were tireless hikers, and we spent the next few days exploring the hills and coastal villages that make up Cinque Terre. We tried local restaurants and found that Mamma Rosa wasn't the only one to guard the sanctity of Ligurian cuisine with an almost religious fervour. Em ordered *fettucine* with smoked salmon and when she asked for grated parmesan, the waiter refused to let her have any.

"Cheese with fish! Absolutely NOT!" he huffed, backing away from our table as though we were unsightly insects.

Returning from the harbour on that first night, we discovered that the bedrooms were co-ed. Em and Tim moved into mine, and a young Italian man joined us. We all took bottom bunks as the top ones had no ladders.

Later, Tim and Em went to the village to make phone calls and the Italian went to the kitchen to chat with Mamma Rosa. I stayed and relaxed in my bunk. Two delicate Japanese women entered, having been assigned the same room. They looked disconcertedly at the top bunks. Just then, I remembered that Tim and Em didn't have a key to get back into the hostel. I hauled myself out of bed, passing the Italian man on my way out. I went and stared sleepily at the front door, wondering if I could somehow leave it ajar for Tim and Em, or if I should just wait for them.

"Excuse me," said a light voice from behind. I turned to see one of the Japanese women. "Are the dorms co-ed?"

"Yes," I answered.

Her eyes opened wide in horror. "Is that why you are out here?"

I wanted to reassure her, tell her that the meeting of cultures and genders can be the true allure of youth hostels, of travel. But I knew she would figure it out for herself, eventually.

She and her friend must have come to bed very late and climbed quietly into the top bunks; we never heard a sound. They were there in the morning, though, wrapped tightly in their sheets, heads covered, still apparently asleep.

On the fifth day, Em and I sat talking over a breakfast of *caffè latte* and *biscotti*. "Come on a trip with me," she said. "Tim is going to Rome to study architecture. I'm heading south for a couple of weeks or so to visit Sorrento. Maybe you can find work there. It'll be fun. What do you say?"

"Where is it?"

"By the sea, south of Naples."

I flinched at the mention of Naples. Back home I had worked at an Italian restaurant to make money for this trip. The manager, a second-generation Neapolitan-Canadian, had given me a warning: "Whatever you do, stay away from Naples." The Camorra, a local Mafia-type organization, played a leading role in his stories. My head was soon filled with images of petty theft at best and murder at worst.

"Naples?" I breathed.

"Yeah, I know," said Em, "but we don't have to stay there. Just long enough to change trains. Sorrento is thirty miles away, a tourist area, totally safe. Come on, it'll be a blast. What have you got to lose?"

I had nothing to lose. I owned only a canvas shopping bag, a pair of Em's cast-off shorts, and the few items I had bought in Germany. I had no job prospects and no definite plans. Malta was in the back of my mind as a possible destination, so south seemed a logical direction to go.

"Okay," I said. "I'll come."

Chapter 5

I wait for the weekends. All the glories of Sorrento pale in comparison to the moment I see Gino after work on Fridays. He is always there to meet me and whisk me off to some fabulous, romantic spot. We visit Caserta, where the royal palace and gardens rival those of Versailles. We picnic and swim on the island of Procida. We take a bus to Assisi, where we wander the medieval streets and admire Giotto's frescoes in the cathedral.

Most weekends, however, we go to Positano, only twenty minutes down the coast and almost visible from my room in Colli di Fontanelle. The *pensione* Gino has found for us is built into the cliff like most structures in Positano. Cool and cavernous with whitewashed walls and spotless tile floors, it provides us with a kitchen, bathroom, and bedroom, and that is all we need.

On Friday evenings, Gino arrives in Sorrento, his pack bursting with olives, *provolone*, wine, and bread. We hurry from the Royal School to the bus, where we snuggle together in the high dark seats that hide us from the few other passengers.

In the summer, this bus is standing room only, but now, in the darkness of a winter evening, we are alone. The bus pitches and sways as we wind our way over the mountain and down the

other side. The moon rises over the Gulf of Salerno, making sil-
houettes of the palms.

This treacherous, twisting road that hangs precariously over
plummeting cliffs once inspired me to gasping, seat-clutching
awe. But now I lean into Gino, his solid strength between me
and the window. We fly high above the star-sparkled sea, pressed
closer together with each swinging curve. Our lives are held by a
thin bus wall, and I have never felt safer.

In Positano, the moon draws us down shadowed stairways,
through tiny cobbled *piazza*s, and past walled terraces until we
reach a tiny *alimentari,* delicatessen. Gino claims the key from the
shopkeeper, and we descend more stairs until we reach our haven.
Gino slides the giant key into the lock, gives it a hefty turn, and
we are in. He unceremoniously dumps the food on the table and
leaves it. "That can wait," he says, as he wraps me in his arms.

Around midnight we emerge from the bedroom, ravenous,
to devour huge chunks of wood-oven-baked bread, great slabs of
provolone, olives by the handful. We use short water glasses for
the wine, as all southerners do.

We hold hands and speak with our eyes. Language lets us
down. There is so much we want to say, and our collective vocabulary is painfully limited. We try a mixture of Italian, English,
and French, with the odd curse word in Neapolitan dialect thrown
in by a frustrated Gino. We manage easily with subjects like the
weather and what we like on our pizza, but expressing our deepest
feelings comes hard. Our hearts will not be patient, will not wait
for our brains to expand. In the end, Gino puts on some Italian
love songs, and we let the music speak for us.

It is in the bedroom of our *pensione* that my mind first regis-
ters what my heart has already understood: Gino is the man from
my dream. In the high-ceilinged room, the memory descends
upon me, and for a moment I am breathless as I watch it shift
into reality. It will be a long time before I dare to bring it into
words. For now it is simply magic and must remain that way. I
hold Gino in silence until we both fall asleep.

Chapter 6

I buy a small guide to the peninsula, complete with well-marked hiking trails. There is a clear red line showing the way from Colli di Fontanelle to Colli di San Pietro, then across the top of the mountain and down to Positano. I figure if I start early in the morning, I'll have plenty of time to catch a bus home before I have to prepare for evening classes at the Royal School.

By the time I reach the base of the mountain at Colli di San Pietro, I realize I'm in for a strenuous hike. The path, barely visible among the prickly brush and sharp rocks, zigzags endlessly up. The day, which started with a clear sky, has clouded over, and the range in front of me is covered in a foggy haze. I consider turning back, but I've come this far and Positano is only a few minutes away by bus, after all.

A little further on, the trail vanishes; there is only the odd paint-splotched rock marking the way. Between one rock and the next, I simply walk in what I think is a logical direction until the next splotch appears, sometimes faded to nothing but the lightest of smudges. And they always do appear, even though the clouds have closed in and I can see only two feet in front of me. There are sheep bells in the distance and droppings nearby, but I find no living creature.

When a hole opens in the fog, I realize I am dangerously close to a precipice, the sea far below, bathed in golden rays of sunshine. The fear of tumbling to my death collides with the intense beauty of the scene. I catch my breath and step carefully back into the haze.

Eventually a path appears, leading down into a chestnut grove. I consult my map and discover I am only halfway there, but I am too focused on the trek to worry about the Royal School schedule.

In the valley of chestnuts, I picnic in a clearing beside the trail, chewing my mozzarella sandwich and relishing the silence. I have been surrounded by noise since I arrived in Italy—motorcycles, motorboats, buses, people shouting, even the crash of waves at Capo. Now, for one blissful moment, there is nothing but my own sounds: the pulse of my blood, the crunch of my teeth. The sandwich revitalizes me, and the earthy scent of the forest brings memories of Canada, of entire days spent alone with nature.

Then comes a shout that makes me jump: "*Cretino! muoviti!* Move it, you idiot!" I jerk around to see a red-faced woodsman beating a mule that is dragging immense bundles of chestnut logs. The mule snorts and gives me a glare in passing, but the man doesn't see me, intent as he is on keeping out of the way of hooves and logs.

After lunch, I walk up the other side of the valley to a small village, which seems to be little more than a depot for chestnut logs that lie in bundles everywhere. I check my map; this village lies directly above Positano and marks the point of descent. There is a clear track here, and I wind my way down towards the shining tiled domes of Positano, which appear gradually larger with each bend.

I am sweating, dirty, and completely exhausted by the time I reach the main road. I refill my water bottle at the fountain and take a long drink. My watch tells me I left home five hours ago. I now have only enough time to hop a bus directly to Sorrento.

No chance to shower or change my clothes at home. I make do with splashing cool water on my face and neck.

A sensation similar to jet lag overcomes me when the bus drops me off in Sorrento in a cloud of exhaust. I look up towards the mountain, still partly covered in fog. It has just taken twenty short minutes to return to another world.

Chapter 7

"Sheila, there is a man watching you from the cliff." Adamo and I are enjoying a snack of hazelnuts and wine in the shelter of our cove. Although it is almost winter, spots like this catch the sun's rays, allowing us to sit comfortably in short sleeves. I follow Adamo's gaze upwards. There is indeed a man, far up on the cliff. He holds binoculars to his eyes, and yes, they seem to be trained on me. Suddenly shivering, I pick up my sweater and drape it over my shoulders.

"*Rattuso*," Adamo breathes. I have never heard this word before, but from Adamo's tone, I can sense exactly what it means. We pack up our things and start the climb to Adamo's house. "Stay for lunch," he says. "We're having spaghetti with mussels. My wife picked them from the cove *'sta mattina*."

"*Grazie*, that would be wonderful."

When we reach the cobbled Roman path through the olive trees, the binocular man is there. Smoking a cigarette, he leans on the terrace wall. He now wears dark glasses, binoculars hanging against his wide chest. He is a big man, balding, the remains of his hair slicked with brilliantine. "*Salve*," he says, using the formal salutation.

"*Salve*," Adamo replies icily, and we continue up the hill. Although I don't turn to look, I sense that the man's gaze follows us. "Don't worry about him," says Adamo. "Just another hopeless *pappagallo*."

We are both a little unnerved, however, and relieved to reach Adamo's solid iron gate set in eight-foot-tall stone walls.

"*Ciao, bella!*" shouts Adamo's wife, Maria, from the kitchen window. "Come on up, lunch is ready!"

Adamo's grandson, Adamo, is there. So is his granddaughter, Maria. I am amazed that they share not only the same house, but the same names as well.

As we're finishing our spaghetti, Adamo's son, Mariano, appears at the door. Unshaven, dirty, carrying a small sack, he looks like a street beggar. The family jumps up to welcome him, demanding he dump the contents of his bag on the table. Maria grabs a large pie plate, and Mariano empties his sack into it. I watch in horror as two dozen tiny dead birds tumble out. Mariano tosses one to the family dog, who crunches it down in two bites, then looks for more.

"Not for you, *goloso*," Adamo says. "These are for our lunch tomorrow." He turns to me. "Have you ever tried *uccellini?*"

I can only shake my head, not sure why anyone would want to kill and eat such delicate creatures. What meat could there possibly be on those sad, miniscule bodies?

"They're a real delicacy," Adamo continues. "You can eat the bones *e tutto*, once they are cooked. So *teneri* and succulent, just crunch them down like Nero here."

The dog looks longingly at the plate as Maria carries it to the fridge. I can't help but be glad I already have plans for lunch the next day.

Adamo walks me to the bus stop. There is no sign of the binocular man. It's been two hours, after all. "He is long gone," says Adamo. "Nothing to worry about."

I kiss him good-bye and board the bus, watching him step sprightly down the path to his paradise by the sea. I am full of mussels, grateful and happy to have spent the afternoon with

friends. Then I glance out the opposite window, and my heart
sinks. The binocular man is there, propped nonchalantly against
a white Fiat, smoking. He waves.

"*Buonasera!*" he calls, less formally this time.

I look away, at the seat in front of me, at the back of the
driver's head. Why isn't this bus moving? Then it rumbles to life,
and I let out a breath I hadn't known I was holding. A couple of
minutes pass before I allow myself to turn and peek out the back
window. He is there, following in his car. I see the shape of his
head framed by dark glasses. I tell myself that he is simply following the bus into Sorrento, as so many cars behind him are doing.
I lose track of him in Sorrento; there is so much traffic, so many
white Fiats.

At Sant'Agnello, the Colli bus is waiting, and I change quickly. It wheezes up, bend after bend until we reach the square. This
is the end of the line. I am the last to get off. "*Buonasera*," says
the driver.

And then I see the man. He is parked on the opposite side of
the square. I run to the house, slam the gate shut, take the steps
two at a time, and arrive at the front door just in time to see him
drive by. I gasp the story to Mamma Russo and her daughter,
Laura.

"*Rattuso*," Mamma hisses, hugging me.

"I'll go get his licence plate number," says Laura. She comes
back a few minutes later. "He must have taken off."

I close the blinds on my windows and keep them that way
all evening.

The next day I see the man in Sorrento, chatting with some
men outside a café. He waves and smiles, like we are friends. I
turn and pretend not to have noticed him, my stomach in knots.
After that, I see him almost daily but not at Capo or Colli, for
which I am grateful; in the town, he begins to seem just one of
the crowd. One day he passes close to me on a narrow sidewalk,
arm in arm with a large blonde woman. His smile in my direction seems to say, "You can relax now." I force myself to smile

back. The woman smiles, too. Adamo was right. Just another *pappagallo*.

Costantino's crush is another matter. Every Monday, Wednesday, and Friday afternoon, he meets my bus in Sant'Agnello, waiting in his little red Fiat *Uno* as I disembark into the square. How much simpler it is to ride comfortably to Sorrento! I no longer have to step over dog turds, fight motor scooters, or inhale deadly fumes. Plus, I am always on time and gaining favour with The Crazy Lady.

But now he insists on driving me home after work, all the way up to Colli. Even if his is the first class of the day, I will surely find him three hours later, outside the school gates. Sometimes he is parked right there in front. Sometimes I catch sight of a flash of red further down the street. Once, I start to walk toward the bus stop, but he pulls up alongside and I hop in without hesitation. He is a gentleman, my student, my only friend in Sorrento.

I enjoy the rides, chatting with him, each of us learning the other's language. I ignore the obvious, that I am leading him on. He knows about Gino, so I fool myself into believing that he is doing all this out of the platonic goodness of his heart. I neglect to ask myself why Gino doesn't know about *him*.

Suddenly he is everywhere. I come out of the fruit shop, the bakery, or a bookstore and there he is, smiling from his car, waving with one hand while the other reaches across to open the passenger door. He is stalking me in his own gentle way.

The evening rides begin to make me uneasy. It is dark after class, the intimacy of his car that much more intense. I try not to listen to the whispers of his cologne. Once, he takes me on a detour through Meta, his village, and we stop for a beer at a *taverna*.

"It's okay," I tell myself. "We're just friends."

But later, on the drive home, he blurts out, "*Sai che mi piaci!*"

There is an awkward silence while my mental dictionary tries to figure out if he said, "You know you like me," or "You know I like you." I'm fairly sure it's the latter.

I blush in the darkness as he deliberately takes the long way up the mountain. I am nervous and guilty. This is the moment of reckoning I must have known would arrive. The fluttering of my heart tells me I have gone too far.

He pulls into the square at Colli and turns off the engine. Night envelops us. Our shoulders are only inches apart in the tiny *Uno*. We make awkward small talk for a few minutes.

"I have to go. I'm expecting a call from Gino," I say, hoping this will once again put us on the firm ground of friendship.

He leans towards me. "Can I kiss you?"

"No," I answer, and then, "I'm sorry."

He ignores this. "Just one kiss?"

"I can't, really," I mumble, reaching for the door handle.

That's when I see Gino. At first I think his image is just a trick of moonlight on glass, but then he is banging on the window, close to my head, towering over the tiny car. His eyes are black with anger. "*La roba sta a casa.*" He turns and strides into the obscurity.

My mind struggles to comprehend. I don't know what *roba* means, and why is he here in Colli on a Thursday evening? I bid a hasty goodnight to Costantino and run to the bus stop where Gino stands, shoulders square, head high, eyes searching for the bus, not for me.

"Don't go!" I plead. "He's just a student who offered me a ride home." I try to make a new truth of the situation, for myself as well as for Gino, but he has already imagined his own.

"And what were you doing for so long in the car?" he accuses.

He had been there at the bus stop the whole time, eyes piercing the night, just able to make out the shape of my blonde head turned towards Costantino's dark one.

What do I say? I hesitate too long. The bus arrives. Panicked, I hug him. "I love you," I whisper into his neck.

His body is rigid. "There are some things for you at the house." He boards the bus and is gone.

Fumes sting my already streaming eyes. Mamma Russo meets me at the door. "Did you see Gino? He was just here ...."

I am sobbing. She puts her arm around me, pulls me into her room, sits me on the bed. Through wads of tissues, I tell only part of the story, the part where I am beyond recrimination.

"How could he just leave like that?" I wonder out loud.

"Gino has overreacted," she says. "He will come to his senses. He will call soon."

For three days I try to convince myself that Gino will call, that he trusts me and loves me enough to let go of his jealousy. I look at the *roba* he dropped off that night: a tie-dyed T-shirt, a hooded bathrobe, a bilingual version of *The Shadow Line*. He made the trek from Naples that evening, just to see me for a few minutes, knowing I return late from work and that the last bus to Naples leaves at eight o'clock.

On the fourth day, I call him. His voice is still cold. Colder even. I instantly know that he had no intention of ever speaking to me again. I press the receiver hard against my ear to stop my hand from trembling. The knowledge that he has thrown it all away, based on one incident, is terrifying. I can think of nothing else but to beg him to meet with me, just to talk.

"*Daccordo*," he says, although I can tell he has decided it will be more of a good-bye than anything else.

I meet him off the train the following day. We walk to a *belvedere*, where we lean on the railing, side by side, but not touching. The bay of Sorrento holds our eyes. Finally turning towards him, I take a breath and tell the safe part of the truth, how nothing happened, how I never wanted anything to happen. I tell him how much I love him, how crazy we would be to end it all. We walk some more, and he tells me about past hurts and pride, about how he would rather give me up than hold less than all my heart. In the end, his eyes soften, and we decide together that without trust, we have nothing. We agree to love each other with absolute confidence and faith. We are okay, although a new small fear tugs at my relief. Later, alone, I reflect on the power of his jealousy, how he was able to harden his heart so quickly, so completely.

I will stand by our agreement, but before I close the door on this horrid episode, I say a silent prayer that I will never regret erasing this small doubt for the future from my mind.

Chapter 8

Gino and I spend our first Christmas apart. My mother is in England at my grandmother's house, so I meet her there. In the original planning, months ago, two weeks seemed like a short time to spend with family, but now it appears a lifetime away from Gino.

I had never been to Liverpool in the winter. The invasive English dampness chills me to the bones like nothing else. There is no sun. And what daylight peeks through the clouds disappears again at two in the afternoon. I survive by staying inside, where warmth and love prevail.

In contrast to the weather outside, my grandmother's house is cozy, welcoming, smelling of buttered toast and tea. At night, I snuggle under quilts my mother used when she was a child, in the room where my mother dreamed her childhood dreams. While the wind whistles outside, she comes to tuck me in, kissing me on the forehead. The years fall away, and I am her little girl again.

My grandmother tells the stories she has always told: stories of growing up on the Isle of Man, of her nursing career, of raising three children through the war. I listen as never before, hanging off every familiar word.

Gino and I speak on the phone, communication made difficult by distance. I need his eyes, his face full of expression, to fully understand the mix of Italian and broken English he uses. We make plans for sun-filled weekends in Positano, walks by the sea, evenings of *amore*.

Saying this second good-bye to my mother is not easy. It is still early days in my travels as well as in my relationship with Gino. How to tell her my plans when I'm not sure of them myself? She lets me go, as she always has, heart surely breaking, a smile on her face as I wave good-bye.

Gino meets me at the airport in Naples. He has borrowed his brother's car so we can go straight to Positano. "Just one stop," he says. "We will pick up your Christmas *regalo*—a scuba mask, snorkel, and flippers."

Never having used such equipment, except for playing in swimming pools, I am dubious. Here there are waves, rocks, and indigo depths full of octopuses and stinging jellyfish.

We go to a diving shop in Naples, where Gino picks out a fluorescent yellow set for me and a similar green set for himself. "We'll be able to snorkel the whole Amalfi Coast," he tells me excitedly.

His past jobs include lifeguard and swimming instructor, so I trust him. I'm just not sure I'll enjoy myself. We'll have to wait until spring to try them out.

My Royal School-imposed budget allows for no extravagance. My gift to Gino is Yeats's *He Wishes for the Cloths of Heaven*, painstakingly copied and decorated by hand, and a large jar of peanut butter brought back from England. I help him translate the first gift, which he loves. The second turns out to be a huge success also; Gino proclaims peanut butter his new favourite sandwich food, especially when paired with *provolone*.

"Do you want to try it with jam or honey?" I ask.

"*Stai scherzando*, are you kidding? This stuff should only be eaten with savoury foods, not sweet ones!"

I try to tell him about PB and J, even banana, but he will hear none of it, popping an olive into his mouth to top off this new taste sensation.

"*Mmmm, delizioso*," he murmurs, rocking back in his chair.

His appetite astounds me. He can polish off half a loaf of dense crusty bread, five or six thick slabs of cheese, ten or twelve olives, and still have room for a second course of salad, salami, and more bread. He falls behind in wine consumption, however. He takes small sips to chase down each monstrous bite, but only while he is eating, up to a two-glass maximum. Half a glass more, and his eyes start to shine and he complains his head is spinning.

"How can you drink three glasses of *vino* and not fall over?" he asks.

I laugh. To be in Italy with Gino is the best gift I could have hoped for.

Chapter 9

In January, I notice that my wages are not covering my expenses. Part-time work at the school just isn't enough to pay for rent, transportation, and food. Although Gino pays for all our weekends, I still fall short.

"Private lessons are the way to go," says Laura, Mamma Russo's eldest daughter. "You can supplement your income from the Royal School and *chissa*, who knows, if it goes well, you can do it full-time."

The idea of being my own boss appeals to me, so I ask Laura to help me write an ad for the paper.

"*Certo*," she says, grabbing a pen and jotting down a few lines. "*Ecco*, there you go. I'll call it in to the paper for you, if you like."

She's already reaching for the phone, so I stop her and ask for a translation of what she has written.

She reads out loud: "Native English speaker available for lessons in your home. Reasonable rates."

I nod my approval and hand the slip of paper back to her. "Sounds fine. Go ahead and make the call."

A few days later, a woman named Arianna contacts me. Her English is already very good, but she wants more practice: "Mostly conversation and some help with idioms and phrasal verbs." She balks when I tell her my fee is twenty thousand lire per hour.

"I was thinking more like ten thousand," she says.

We settle on fifteen thousand for the first lesson. I suggest a two o'clock appointment, so I can go straight to the Royal School afterwards. She hesitates a moment, then agrees to the time. She gives me directions to her apartment in Sant'Agnello, right across from my usual bus stop.

"See you tomorrow at two o'clock," I confirm.

"Yes ... alright," she hesitates again.

Before hanging up, I hear a man's voice muttering in the background.

I arrive at Arianna's gate at five to two, and push the button labelled *Avvocato Francone*, Lawyer Francone, as she instructed. The gate clicks open; she must have seen me coming. The court- yard is full of flowering plants and cats. I am about to buzz again at her door when it opens and she greets me with a smile and a handshake. Arianna is tall and slim, about my age and dressed in a floral print dress that is both shapely and flowing. Raven hair cascades down her back. I find her stunning and exotic, a complete contrast to the image I had of a dowdy housewife in flip-flops and housedress. She doesn't look Italian, and I wonder where she is from.

She invites me into a small *salotto*, which is lined on one side from floor to ceiling with bookcases full of books, hundreds of them in various languages. There is also a desk with a computer on it and a red velvet couch. A tiny balcony overlooks the noisy street and the bus stop. A doorway between the bookcases leads to an office, where I glimpse a large carved desk and chair.

"*Arianna, chi è?*" calls a man's voice.

"*È l'insegnante, la canadese,*" she calls back.

Then the *Avvocato* Ciro Francone appears in the doorway. He is tall and imposing, with a striking resemblance to Marcello Mastroianni. "*Piacere,*" he says, holding out his hand and bow-ing, either formally or mockingly at the waist. "So you're the one who insists on disturbing a workingman's *controra*."

I am taken aback, but then I see the twinkle in his eye and know that he is only half serious. I had completely forgotten about the sacred *controra*, that siesta period of two or three hours post-lunch, when most of southern Italy is at rest, digesting, snoozing, or making love.

"Don't mind him," says Arianna. "This is a perfect time for lessons. It's quieter, and I certainly had no other plans. Ciro can do his lawyerly thing in the other room." They stare each other down for a moment, and then the *Avvocato* Francone turns back to his office.

"*Buona lezione*," he says over his shoulder.

Our lesson turns out to be immensely enjoyable for both of us. While we talk about ourselves, I correct her usage, which is practically flawless, and introduce a few idioms for her to practise. Arianna works mainly from home as a translator and Spanish teacher. The daughter of a Spanish mother and an Italian father, Arianna lived much of her life in Bilbao, where she was known as *l'italiana*.

"Now that I am in Italy, everyone calls me *la spagnola*," she laughs. "I am happy living here with Ciro, but I miss Bilbao, where I never had to worry about the neighbours gossiping behind my back. Ciro and I are not married, so many of the locals here consider me little more than a *puttana*. They only pretend to treat me with respect because Ciro is a lawyer."

We talk easily, sharing stories; the hour flies by. At three o'clock, I accept her original offer of ten thousand lire because I already consider her a friend and am embarrassed to ask for twenty thousand or even fifteen thousand for such easy work. Arianna, on the other hand, is so thrilled to have met me, someone with whom she can truly converse, that she insists on paying me the full twenty thousand. We end up anti-bargaining and finally settle once again on fifteen thousand lire.

Soon, Arianna and I are close friends. Our teacher-student

relationship expands to include shopping and lunches. One day, returning from the market, Arianna spots a woman waving from the bus stop. She nudges me and whispers, "That's Teresa, she's recently married and finding life away from her parents more difficult than she had expected."

Arianna introduces me to her friend, who shakes my hand, then immediately starts, "*Dio mio,* Arianna, how do you manage? It's killing me, trying to keep up with the daily shopping, cooking, cleaning, laundry, and ironing. This damn bus is late. If I don't get lunch on the table by one o'clock, Giovanni will be *furioso,* and my whole schedule for the afternoon will be thrown off."

Arianna doesn't even blink once: "Cook twice as much as you need each time, then save half for the next meal or the next day. Make it into a *frittata* or *zuppa.* As for ironing, I do most of it on the weekends when I have more time. I do the heavy housecleaning then, too."

I listen, fascinated. True, Ciro is a lawyer and certainly needs freshly pressed shirts every day, but to sacrifice a weekend seems drastic. I think of Gino, who wears T-shirts and sweatpants to his job in the glove factory, who doesn't notice the dust bunnies under the bed, and loves to cook when he has the chance.

Aren't Saturdays and Sundays meant for exploring hidden coves or for hiking cool mountain paths under the shade of Mediterranean pines? What would a weekend be without picnics, adventures, and discoveries? I keep these thoughts to myself, but later, over tea at Arianna's house, I suggest introducing Ciro and Gino to each other. "We could spend some time together on the weekend, maybe go for a walk or something."

We speculate on whether Ciro and Gino will get along or whether their differences will make friendship impossible.

Arianna calls the following day to say that Ciro would like to take Gino and me to *la pineta,* the pine forest, to pick mushrooms. "He says that since you are both foreign to the area, he would be pleased to show you some of the hidden treasures."

We laugh. I know, from what Arianna has told me, that Ciro is fiercely *campanilista*, proud of his region, but I can't believe he would call someone from Naples a foreigner! I'm afraid Gino might be turned off by his arrogance.

From the moment they meet, however, Gino and Ciro hit it off. They begin by being overly polite, using gracious gestures and formal speech, until they establish that there is, in fact, a ground from which to build. Soon they are joking in dialect, Gino welcoming Ciro's wealth of information on everything from smoked ham to cars.

Ciro is surprised by how familiar we already are with the peninsula. He flips through my guidebook of trails, nodding in appreciation. "Sheila, I can't believe you discovered places I have never seen, even before you met Gino." His admiration is tinged with disapproval, however, as he rarely lets Arianna out of his sight and certainly would never condone her traipsing across mountainsides by herself.

"Now remember," lectures Ciro, ushering us into his classic BMW, "to find mushrooms, you must think like a mushroom. Anyone can stumble upon the proliferous *boletus*, but it takes true *funghi*-sense to sniff out the *lactarius*, which conceals itself under dense grassy tufts."

Up, up, up we toil to the top of Mount Lattari, the highest point at this end of the peninsula. We pass through Colli di Fontanelle, up through chestnut groves, then turn onto a narrow paved track that leads to the World Wildlife Fund forest. Ciro parks the car near the entrance, and we get out. A tiny forest by Canadian standards, perhaps one mile long and half a mile wide, it is an oasis of cool breezes singing and sighing through pine needles.

I close my eyes for a moment and am once again transported to the forests of my childhood, where I took silence and fresh air for granted. This is a special place, man-made and managed, but developed differently from the rest of the peninsula.

Ciro's voice breaks the silence: "A motion has been made

to raze *la pineta* and turn it into a golf course, for tourists, of course, since southern Italians couldn't care less for the sport. So far, there has been no progress in this direction, so we hope it will never come to pass."

Arianna, dressed for the occasion in tight beige pants and high black boots, unloads a large straw basket from the trunk of the car. There are other people hunting mushrooms today, mostly *vecchi*, old men and women hunched and drably dressed, their plastic bags and baskets bulging with *funghi*.

"*Venite*," says Ciro, pulling several walking sticks from the trunk. "I will show you a good place."

We start along the main trail, a wide swathe cut straight from one end of the forest to the other. There is some fitness equipment here and there, ropes and pulleys and benches and ladders. "Lots of young people come here to run and exercise," says Ciro. "The *vecchi* come for the *funghi*."

The walking sticks are not really for walking, but for poking. Ciro shows us how to gently move the bushy strands of dry grass and pine needles aside with the stick, so we can peek underneath without bending over. We spend an hour happily picking what we find, always presenting our specimens for Ciro's approval. As it turns out, I have a knack, some kind of innate mushroom-divining sense that leads me to all the best spots. Before long, we have enough for a decent meal. I can see that Gino is dying to try out the exercise equipment and go for a run, but Ciro and Arianna are focused solely on lunch, so we leave. I know Gino will be back the first chance he has.

In Colli di Fontanelle, Ciro makes a detour down a small lane, parking the car close to a guardrail on a high hill of lush greenery that plunges before us into the sea.

"I know the man who owns this property," says Ciro. "I come here to pick wild chard."

We step over the guardrail onto a well-worn path.

"*Vedete*," Ciro points, "see how thick the *erbe* grow in this place." He pulls a plastic bag and a knife from his pocket, grasps a handful of leafy plants, and slices them off close to the roots.

Arianna rubs her hands in glee. "Ooh, I'll make a *frittata* to have with our mushrooms."

"We can use this, too," Ciro says as he picks some bright green fronds.

"What is it?" I ask.

"I think you call it wild fennel in English," says Arianna. "Here, have a sniff."

The plant smells wonderful, like licorice and fresh air after rain.

Gino, eager to contribute, insists we stop at my place to pick up the bread he brought from Naples. Ciro is skeptical that any bread could be better than that found on the peninsula, but he parks outside Mamma Russo's house while I dash inside to retrieve the giant loaf.

"This is *pane cotto a fascine*, baked in a very hot wood-burning oven, made with a darker grain than regular bread," explains Gino. He sees Ciro's doubtful face and laughs confidently. "Wait 'til you taste it!"

Back at the apartment, we gather around the kitchen table to sort through the mushrooms, chard, and fennel. Ciro chooses the plumpest mushrooms, cleans them, and chops them ready for frying. Arianna takes the leafy tops from the chard, washes them, and throws them into a frying pan with oil, garlic, and some sprigs of fennel. Instead of discarding the stems of the chard, she dips them into flour and beaten egg, then fries them in a separate pan. While the stems are browning, she dumps the fried leaves into more egg, then pours the mixture back into the pan.

The meal is prepared so quickly, minutes later we are sitting down to battered chard stems and leaf *frittata* while the mushrooms, our second course, simmer on the stove. Ciro pours wine, Gino slices the whole loaf of bread, and we dig in. Ciro, mouth full, gestures approvingly with the bread, and Gino beams. When the mushrooms are cooked, Arianna serves them just as they are so we can taste their fresh earthiness untainted by other flavours.

"To *la penisola sorrentina*," says Ciro, "the land of plenty."

We toast the bounty of the region, then we toast our new friends.

"What about the bread?" asks Gino.

"*Allora, si*," says Ciro. "Next weekend, when you come, a loaf wouldn't be unwelcome."

Chapter 10

Winter catches up with me at the end of January. The rainy season has come and, although the temperature is still above zero, positively balmy by Canadian standards, I cannot keep warm. Adamo's family has given me sweaters, wool skirts, shoes, and a coat. I am constantly layered. Even in bed, where the heavy blankets press me so far into the mattress I can hardly move, I wear two pairs of socks, wool leggings, and a hooded sweater. Figaro, the Russo cat, sleeps on my feet. As Laura says, he is better than a hot-water bottle because he never goes cold.

In the mornings, the clouds are so thick around the mountain I can see nothing from the window except the balcony railing. At the bus stop, I shelter from the drizzle, but by the time we reach Sant'Agnello, the sun is often shining and the layers start to find their way into my pack. But sometimes it is raining there, too. People huddle in cafés, only venturing out when absolutely necessary. Motor scooter traffic is greatly reduced. Many students don't show up for class, using the poor weather as an excuse. My feet are constantly wet. Even Positano is cool and damp, our umbrellas brushing against the narrow passageways where the stairs have become wild splashing torrents.

A landslide near Castellamare cuts the peninsula off from

Naples. Work crews manage to clear the road in a couple of days, but one of the train tunnels is badly damaged and rail travel becomes impossible. Commuters without cars are forced to take the infrequent and expensive hydrofoil. After a few days, buses are brought in to carry train passengers around the crumbling tunnel to another train waiting on the other side. The fifty-minute trip now takes close to two hours. Julio and The Crazy Lady try it, give up immediately, and begin using the hydrofoil. Gino perseveres on the train, leaving Naples earlier on Friday and going home later on Sunday so we can spend the same precious time together.

Then the flu hits. Mamma Russo gets it first and recovers just in time to look after the rest of us. I hope my strong Canadian constitution will spare me, but the day after Laura and her brother fall ill, I awake in the night with that fear of vomiting I remember from my childhood. I want desperately to go back to sleep and forget it, but I know that the cold bathroom floor is the only place I'm going to spend the next hours. Mamma Russo comes and soothes me back to bed. In the morning, she brings me scented tea and some medicine. I have no idea what she is making me swallow, but I trust her. I sleep most of the day and feel much better by evening.

The next day is a Friday, so I call in sick, just to be safe. Losing a day's work is one thing, but I can't bear to miss my weekend with Gino. We take the bus to Positano as usual, but I am still weak and light-headed. The weather is kind, however, and we spend the days lazing on the beach and strolling slowly along the coast trail. There are no midnight feasts or lovemaking. After dinner I simply fall asleep in the bedroom of our *pensione*, Gino's warm body spooned around mine.

In February, frigid winds begin to whistle over the mountain, under the French doors, and through the large diagonal crack in the window. Rolled in a *cannellone* of wool blankets, I sleepily remember winter storms. A wind like this means large snowdrifts are piling up outside. Frozen landscapes fill my dreams until morning. When daylight comes, I emerge from my cocoon to peer over the balcony.

There are oranges everywhere. Drifts of them in the village square, in the fountain, squashed in the middle of the road, wedged between the slats of the goat-shed roof. The scent of fresh-squeezed orange juice rises to my nostrils. I stare with early-morning eyes, struggling to process this image. But there it is in larger-than-life Technicolour: February in southern Italy. A gift I never expected to receive.

From scorching November days to freezing torrential rains, from the punctual afternoon *Maestrale* to the astonishing African *Scirocco*, weather on the peninsula is constantly amazing. My first encounter with the *Scirocco* takes me truly by surprise one February day. The sky turns an eerie yellow, but the breeze is unusually summery. A perfect day to hang out my laundry. How odd that no one else has theirs out, I think.

Later, when I go to collect my dry clothes, I find out why. They are covered in sand. Sand from the Sahara, carried on the wind across the sea, Gino explains when I lament. How extraordinary! I imagine the exotic origins of these golden grains. Perhaps I will find the odd camel hair stuck to my socks.

The romance subsides as I realize I will have to wash and dry my clothes a second time. Surely a few laughs have been had at my expense, but I don't really mind. If I never have the chance to visit Africa, at least I can say that Africa visited me!

Chapter 11

"V*ieni,* Sheila!" shrieks Mamma Russo through my kitchen door. "If you've nothing else to do, we'll go to Castellamare Terme together. The water there is *magnifica.*"

I put down my *Italianissimo* textbook, quickly grab my pocket dictionary, and look up *terme*. Spa, it says. So I throw my bathing suit and a towel in a bag and follow her outside. Mamma opens the passenger door of her Fiat 500, affectionately known as Topolino, Mickey Mouse. "*Sali, Sali!*" she shouts.

I wonder why she's calling me Sally and hesitate just a moment. She says it again, more emphatically: "*Sali! Devi salire,* Sheila!"

I get it. The second person of the verb *salire*, "to go up," must also be used for "get in" where cars are concerned. And it happens to sound just like the name Sally. We squeeze ourselves into the car. Mamma's girth is crushed up against the steering wheel and my knees are pressed against the dashboard even though the seats are back as far as they will go. Laura gives the car a push to start us off down the hill. We reach the coastal highway, puttering under the mountain range through two smog-choked tunnels.

Mamma seems oblivious to the other drivers tearing past until one cuts us off and she screams, "*Scemo!*" at the top of her well-practised lungs. I jump in my seat, banging my head on the roof of Topolino. The word remains seared into my brain, and I look it up later: "Idiot," of course. What else would it be?

At Castellamare, we park on the main street near the harbour. Mamma opens the trunk and hauls out four glass demijohns and two crates full of empty water bottles. "Help me carry these down to the *sorgente*," she says.

More than a spring, it is four taps built into a cement wall, pouring water constantly into a stone basin. People are lined up with their own crates and demijohns. When our turn comes, I hand Mamma bottle after bottle as she fills and corks each one. "*Vedrai*," she pants as we transport our cargo back to the car. "You'll see. This is the best water in all of Italia. A glass of this with your *pranzo*, and you will experience perfect digestion!"

Later, when I mention this phenomenon to Gino, he confirms Mamma's story.

"Ah yes, the water of Castellamare is *famosa*. It's exported throughout the world under the name *Acqua della Madonna*. It is considered a very healthful mineral water, almost *frizzante* in taste. Very special. I often make the trip from Napoli as it is my mother's favourite water."

Bottles packed neatly into the trunk, we return to Sorrento. I realize that 'spa' was not quite the word I had been looking for. I add "larger dictionary" to my mental list of things to buy. In Sorrento we stop outside a fruit shop I recognize from my days at the youth hostel. "I just need to pick up some *peperoni*," Mamma breathes, dislodging herself from the steering wheel.

"They don't sell any here!" I call, but the traffic drowns my voice. When she comes back with a bag full of red peppers, I'm glad she didn't hear me.

"*Ecco dei bei peperoni*," she says, tossing them into the back. Another new word. Who needs to stay at home studying when a trip with Mamma can provide so much vocabulary?

"One more stop," she announces, maneuvering around the

block and parking in front of a hardware store. "*Una stufa per la tua stanza.*"

I follow her inside, trying to guess what a *stufa* might be. She quickly selects a gas heater on wheels for my room. I'm relieved to have this problem resolved. The winter winds are blowing colder every day. We cram this last purchase into the back seat and toil up the mountain.

After we unload the car, Mamma says, "*Vieni, è ora per La Ruota Della Fortuna.*"

The Wheel of Fortune is Mamma's favourite television program, and I am pleased to be invited into her bedroom for this evening ritual. She pulls on her woollen hat and nestles her bulk against the pillows. The Russos have no living room, only three bedrooms, a bathroom, and a kitchen, so Mamma's room houses the TV and the kids often join her, under the blankets or seated on the bed.

I sit on the edge and await my next lesson. "*Compro la A di Ancona*, I'd like to buy an A for Ancona," says the contestant. Whenever a letter is named, so is the corresponding city. I recite this alphabet to myself, trying to pronounce each city with the correct accent: *la B di Bari, la C di Como, la D di Domodossola....*

Once *The Wheel of Fortune* is over, I bid Mamma *buona notte* and retire to my room. My *Italianissimo* text lies open at *Passato Prossimo e Remoto*. I close it, not bothering to mark the page. Instead, I fall into bed, where I dream of mineral *sorgenti* flowing through the town of Ancona, while red and yellow *peperoni* roast over a gas *stufa....*

Chapter 12

"Why hasn't Gino introduced you to his parents?" Adamo wants to know.

I'm not sure how to answer. Gino and I have been together for three months, and he still balks at the idea of taking me home. "My parents have never respected my privacy," Gino told me. "This is one part of my life I want to keep *segreta*, for just a little longer." He didn't say it, but I know he is worried that they will find a foreigner unsuitable for their son. Neapolitan mammas are notoriously protective. I want his mother to love me. How will I feel if she treats me with rancour or disdain?

An only child myself, I am dying to meet his three brothers and two sisters. I'm curious about how Gino and his brothers all work together in the family glove factory. I want to know where he lives, see where he eats and sleeps, meet his nieces and nephews. I listen avidly when he tells me how all the brothers used to share the same room, how they took turns getting up in the night to nurse their dying grandmother.

Now there is only Gino and his youngest sister, Ornella, at home. Ornella has a *fidanzato,* so she is expected to marry soon. Roberto, the youngest son, has an apartment nearby but comes to the family house for lunch, to take showers, and to drop off his laundry.

The Confalone *casa*, Gino tells me, is located close to the factory, just a couple of blocks away. The boys all join their father at home for lunch, squeezing around the kitchen table for a *primo* of pasta, a *secondo* of meat or fish, wine, and bread, and always espresso to top off the meal and aid digestion. A short rest and it's back to the factory, where Gino works the enormous iron *pressa*, pulling a handle the size of a human leg to slice shapes of hand, fingers, and thumb through stacks of fabric. The main products they turn out are *fodere*, linings, mostly silk, ready to be sold to the leather glove manufacturers. But they also make velvet, satin, and other fabric gloves. Gino has already given me several pairs of sumptuous velvet in rich purple, autumn red, and turquoise.

I don't push him for the family introduction. He will take me to his home one day. How could he not? We are in love. We talk of a future together, here or perhaps in Canada. For Gino is curious too. I tell him about the open spaces, about never seeing your neighbours if you don't want to, about the changing of the leaves in autumn and snow that falls for days on end, covering everything in a glistening blanket. From a distance, it is easy to romanticize. At the moment, location is only our backdrop. Together is where we want to be.

"I am the most important part of Gino's life," I tell Adamo. "He loves me. That's all that matters for now. The rest will come."

"And what about you?" he demands. "Are you truly serious about him? Are you ready to give up your homeland to make a life here with Gino? For you know you could never take him to live in Canada. A *napoletano* does not transplant well."

I remind him of the thousands of Neapolitans who did just that after the Second World War.

"Ah, but are they *contenti*?" he wonders. "Or do they dream every night of the land they left behind?"

Chapter 13

Sundays in Positano we lie in bed until late, listening to the church bells toll for others. Then we breakfast in a café, ordering *cornetti*, croissants filled with apricot jam, and cappuccino at the bar as all locals do. Tables are for tourists who don't know or don't care that the same food eaten sitting down costs double.

Gino's *cornetto* is gone in two bites, his cappuccino in two gulps. He is always precise; the number of bites must equal the number of gulps. Otherwise, his whole day is thrown off. I learned early never to offer him the last piece of my croissant after he has finished. He can't eat it without a coffee chaser, but he can't bear to waste it, either. His grandmother taught him that throwing away anything related to bread is akin to tossing the body of Christ in a dumpster.

Once, he found a crust left from some past lunch of mine, dried up and forgotten in the bottom of my bag. "We must save this for croutons," he declared, wrapping it in a napkin and placing it carefully in his pocket.

Now I know that I must calculate my own hunger quotient and offer him the piece I won't eat *before* he finishes. That way, he can adapt the size of his gulps to accommodate an extra bite.

Today, Gino waits as I finish the foam from my cappuccino

with a spoon. When the last sweet mouthful is gone, I smile at him. "Shall we head back to the *pensione* and prepare our picnic for the day?" I ask.

He clears his throat. "I was thinking we could go to *casa mia* for lunch."

"Are you serious? To your parents' house?"

"*Sì, che dici*, what do you say?"

"But isn't it terribly short notice? We should have called."

"We can call now. Notice doesn't matter. My mother always prepares a big lunch on Sundays. Two more won't make a difference."

I think it will make all the difference in the world, but I let Gino call the shots. This is a big step for him.

While he calls his mother from a pay phone outside the café, I mentally sort through the clothes that lie strewn around the bedroom of the *pensione*. I have little to wear at the best of times. On Positano weekends, I have even less.

"*Ce verimmo aroppo*," he says in dialect, then hangs up.

I question with my eyes, and he replies, "It's all set. Lunch is at one o'clock."

"Can we stop in Colli so I can put on something decent?" I ask, afraid he will say we must go straight to Naples.

"Sure, if you like."

Since Gino cares less than anyone I know about clothes, this answer is far less casual than it seems. His parents' first impression of me is going to count for a lot.

In Colli, I choose a black wool skirt and black sweater with green stripes. I am learning to dress dark. My bright yellow windbreaker and red day pack lie untouched in the dim recesses of the colossal wardrobe. I opt instead for a grey jacket and an imitation leather bag I picked up for a few lire in Sorrento. I brush my hair and put on a little makeup. "How do I look?"

"*Perfetta*. You are perfect in every way," he says, trying to convince us both.

I am Canadian, a *straniera*. I might lure their son away to an icy land full of wild animals and loose women. I have spent the past weekends doing god-knows-what out of wedlock with their son. His mother could easily consider me no better than the *bambole* she watches on soaps like *Beautiful* and *Beverly Hills.*

"Let's go," I say. "We don't want to miss the bus down to Sant'Agnello."

Although I am nervous, I enjoy the train ride, comfortable in Gino's presence. One glaring glance from Gino and the lascivious stares of other men slide abruptly off my blonde head and onto the grimy floor.

From Stazione Centrale, it's a hair-raising half-hour walk to Gino's house. This is not the picturesque centre of Naples; the road we are following lies under a long highway overpass. I hold Gino's hand, almost jogging to keep up with his quick pace. He instinctively incorporates the avoidance of dog turds into his step. My eyes are constantly downcast, but there is little view to appreciate anyway: street-side gas stations, grimy hardware stores, dark shops with barred windows.

The sidewalk disappears, and the two-lane street becomes one-and-a-half lanes as we pass through an ancient tunnel. We press ourselves crablike against the filthy walls as cars roar through in both directions. I hold my breath against the fumes. We emerge into even more traffic. Two wide streets intersect here, but it seems like more; cars are tearing in all directions at once, with no traffic lights, of course. We dodge our way across the street in a bizarre dance with traffic; Neapolitan drivers are heavy on the accelerator, but they are quick with the brake, too. I expect to hear the crunch of metal, or worse, of our bones, but the drivers are espresso-alert, avoiding us and each other with absolute finesse.

We hurry past more shops, wares spilling onto the sidewalk, then when we reach a bust of Caruso mounted on a pedestal, Gino turns abruptly into a narrow side street. A small shrine to the *Madonna del Carmine*, fresh flowers at her feet, welcomes us to the *quartiere*, the neighbourhood the Confalone family calls home.

The apartment buildings are not tall, perhaps six stories maximum, but the narrowness of the street makes them seem to tower above us. Laundry hangs from every balcony, sometimes right across the street. Sheets and tea towels wave like flags at a racetrack. *Motorini* dart around us, unimpeded by parked cars or sidewalks.

Gino's building is barricaded by a sturdy metal door. *"Apri,"* he says into the intercom, and the door pops open. The foyer is wide, mailboxes lining the walls. There is a concierge's booth, which has long been empty save for layers and layers of dust. We walk up to the *primo piano*, first floor, which to me is actually the second floor. Gino's mother is at the door, arms open. Gino hugs and kisses her, then she does the same to me. She smells of garlic and basil and strongly resembles Gino. I see no malice in her eyes.

"Vieni, vieni," she says, taking my hand and leading me into the large *salotto*.

Gino's father is there, watching a soccer game full blast on TV. He is thin and grey, but there is an elegant pride about him. *"Benvenuta,* Sheila," he says in a voice so soft it is drowned out by the television.

Then he sits silently as Signora Confalone bombards me with questions. I do not feel invaded, however. She is warm and genuinely curious about me, about Canada, about my family. Gino keeps reminding her to speak Italian rather than dialect. I struggle to answer, looking to Gino for help. Gino's father is almost deaf; when I think I have perfectly enunciated a simple reply, he turns to Gino for translation: *"Cosa ha detto?"*

"She said she has no brothers or sisters!" shouts Gino in dialect.

Every once in a while, Signor Confalone's attention is drawn to the game on TV. The volume splits my head.

"It's impossible to talk in here," says Gino. "Let's go into the kitchen."

His mother follows, pulling out a chair for me at the table.

"Would you like a glass of *vino, acqua, aranciata*…?" she asks, rummaging through various bottles on the counter. I think that maybe she is nervous, too.

"A glass of *acqua, per favore*."

Gino sits down beside me. "My father won't admit he's going deaf. He has the *televisione* on so loud it drives the rest of us crazy."

"Soon the others will be here, and we will *mangiare*," says his mother.

I wonder how many of Gino's five brothers and sisters will be coming today, but when I look questioningly at him, he just shrugs.

The tiny kitchen is steaming with sauces, boiling water, and various *fritture*.

"Try some *mulignane a fungetiell*," says Gino's mother, passing me a plate of purplish cubes swamped in tomato sauce. They are slightly chewy. I recognize garlic, oil, and basil, the base ingredients of most Neapolitan dishes.

"*Delizioso*," I say, scooping some more onto a slice of bread. "What is it?"

"*Mulignane a fungetiell*," she says, slightly louder this time.

"They are chunks of eggplant *fritti* in olive oil, then stewed in tomato sauce," Gino explains. "My mother has many recipes for eggplant, all *magnifiche*."

He smiles at his mother, and she embraces him, unconditional love flowing from her every pore.

The buzz of the intercom announces the arrival of Gino's eldest brother, Gennaro, his wife, Anna, and their two sons, Angelo and Francesco. The boys explode into the kitchen. "*Nonna! Nonna!*" they shout. "What's for lunch? We're starving!" Then they catch sight of me and are momentarily struck dumb.

"This is Sheila, Gino's *fidanzata*," says Signora Confalone.

The word *fidanzata* makes me slightly uncomfortable. It is freely used to mean "serious girlfriend," although it translates as "fiancée." But then I am glad she has referred to me as "serious" and not simply as *ragazza*, plain old casual girlfriend.

When Gennaro and Anna come in, the kitchen is at capacity. Gennaro is handsome like Gino, but his Confalone features are hidden behind a beard and mustache. He is slightly shorter, too, and walks with a limp, having suffered from polio as a child. Gino has told me the story: there were no decent health services in Naples, so the family was forced to look elsewhere. They found a clinic in France, but the expense meant they lived hand to mouth for many years.

Anna is small boned, with striking features and long curly hair. Her large eyes and mouth are accented by bright makeup. She and Gennaro kiss me. Again, I feel no judgement, only warmth.

"Nice to finally meet you," says Gennaro, eyes laughing in Gino's direction. Then he and the boys head to the TV, while Anna applies an apron and busies herself at the stove. The women laugh together, chattering in dialect, and I am lost again.

Gino takes me to see the rest of the apartment. I can't believe a family of nine lived here. Gino and his brothers and sisters slept in the *salotto*. I know that Gino now has it to himself at night, sleeping on the pull-out couch, but there is no sign of his things. His clothes, pillow, sheets, books and CDs are neatly stored away in cupboards and wardrobes throughout the house. Instead, there is a dining room table, chairs, the TV, and shelves full of *bomboniere*. The spotless tile floor reflects light from a window and French doors, the latter leading onto a tiny balcony that overlooks the noisy street. I imagine the room full of beds, youngsters pillow fighting or wrestling on the hard floor.

I remember my own room in Canada. The domain of an only child, it was overflowing with everything I owned: magazines, books, clothes, makeup, shoes, posters of teen idols. There was barely room to step from the doorway to the bed. And hidden under the bed were more of my precious possessions, commingled with dust balls and cat hairs.

Gino's grandmother had the small bedroom that now belongs to Gino's youngest sister, Ornella. The other bedroom belongs to his parents. There is one full bathroom and another smaller one with a shower, toilet, and mini washing machine the size of a bar fridge.

The kitchen glistens immaculately, every inch of cupboard and counter utilized. French doors open onto the balcony, which in this mild climate is used as an extension of the kitchen. Bottles of water, preserved tomatoes, eggplant, and artichokes line shelves in the corner. There is also a freezer, a sink, and a canary in a cage.

This is the courtyard side of the building. Neighbours are everywhere: to the right, left, above, below, and across. I have to crane my neck to see the sky. An airplane flies overhead. We are only several miles from the airport, but the noise is barely distinguishable from the prevailing pandemonium that is Naples.

The reverberation of the intercom brings us back inside. Gino's brother Ettore has arrived with his wife, Antonella, and their six-year-old son, Lorenzo. The kitchen is suddenly full again. Ettore hugs his mother, towering over her, over us all. His mustachioed smile stands a good six inches above Gino's head. Antonella is small and elegant, with short hair and subtle makeup. And while Angelo and Francesco are surprisingly light haired, Lorenzo is dark, a Confalone through and through. He is quiet by Antonella's side as she, too, welcomes me into the family.

Then, out of nowhere, Ornella appears, squeezing through the doorway past Ettore. "*Ciao,* Sheila, *ma come sei bella!*" she exclaims, commenting on my appearance with typical southern openness.

I find her *bella,* too. She is slight, with long, straight chestnut hair; her face is striking, not just for its beauty, but for its likeness to Gino's. Missing are Roberto and Elena. Roberto is single, but Elena is married with two teenage children. The walls must burst when all of them get together.

This is enough for one day. I am completely overwhelmed by

the sheer quantity of people. My mother's family is in England; my father has one half-sister remaining in his. For as long as I can remember, family has been just me and my parents.

Anna, Antonella, and Ornella are helping to prepare lunch and set the table. I offer to pitch in, but they insist that I am the guest of honour and must just relax and enjoy. When all the men, children, and I are seated around the table in the *salotto*, the women start to bring in huge slabs of lasagna. They serve themselves smaller portions, but as the guest, I must have a full plate. They don't really expect me to eat it all and are not offended when I pass more than half my serving to Gino.

Next comes a whole fish with salad. Glassy eyes stare up from my plate, and I hurriedly cut off the head and hide it under a lettuce leaf. The fish is light, cooked in herbs and white wine. I eat all of it.

The third course is a roast of lamb baked in the oven with potatoes, onions, and peas. Gino receives almost all of mine. He scoops it up with bread, sopping each last drop from his plate. A platter of salami, *prosciutto*, and cheese is passed around, and then comes dessert. Ornella has prepared *tiramisù*, dripping with *mascarpone* and espresso. I can't resist. I wish I had Gino's stomach. As the last bite melts in my mouth, Gino's mother brings me an espresso, for digestive purposes.

I cannot move. The TV is still on, has been throughout the meal, and the men are now glued to it. The children, finished after the second course, play soccer in the hall.

"*Calmatevi!*" shouts Gennaro as the ball flies into the room, ricocheting off a cabinet full of *bomboniere*.

I insist on helping to clear the table and when this task is completed, the inquisition begins again. Having lived all their lives in Naples, the family is curious about life in Canada. I tell them that yes, there are mountains and oceans, but these things are as far away from my home as England is from Italy. There are lakes you can't see across and a winter that lasts six months of the year. We go outside in temperatures below zero and don't die of exposure. I am an only child, and my parents let me leave, gave me their blessing.

"*Interessante,*" they murmur, eyes wide in disbelief.

Afterwards, Gino takes me to the factory, just a block away. He shows me the *pressa* that was built by his great-uncle, the basement full of roll upon roll of exquisite fabrics, the cutting tables, and the sewing machines. It is a dark place with only one small window. There are exposed pipes on the ceiling and years of fabric dust on the floor.

"This is where my father worked, and my grandfather. Napoli was once the glove capital of the world. Now things are changing. Competition from Asia is very *forte*, and we are having trouble keeping up. The quality of our gloves is unmatched, but we cannot sell them cheaply."

I can feel the history here. I want to know more, but Gino says it is time to go and bid good-bye to his family.

Everyone crowds around for three kisses each. I lose track of how many lips touch my cheek. "*Ciao, bella!*" they shout as we head down the stairs to the lobby. My head is reeling with noise, wine, and intimate contact with so many strangers.

"It's late," says Gino. "I will accompany you on the train to Sorrento." This means he will spend hours in transit, with tomorrow a workday. He will not hear my protestations. "You have no idea of the *gente* who travel at night. The train will likely be full of thieves and drug addicts."

We sit close to the driver's cabin, the safest place according to Gino. We look out the train window into the night, into our own image superimposed on the passing towns and villages. What makes a family, I wonder. I will certainly never be a Neapolitan, for there is no Spanish, Greek, or Roman blood mixed with mine. But will I one day don an apron in the Confalone kitchen? Will I joke easily like Anna and Antonella do, in a language I as yet barely understand? These unknowns are too much for my tired brain to consider. What I do know is that while the depth of my feelings for Gino remains the same, the breadth has increased immensely.

Chapter 14

When I am alone for too long, when the wind and rain keep me inside, I torment myself with thoughts of home. Home, where I understand the language. Home, where I can go about my business and not be stared at, followed, or questioned. I dream of a life with no work permits, draughty bedrooms, or motor scooters. I imagine what it would be like to show Gino my parents' country home, surrounded by one hundred acres of silent forest and farmland. I want him to experience the atmosphere of a winter's evening by the fireplace, snow falling soundlessly outside, quiet music on the stereo. We would recline on the sofa, my head nestled on his shoulder, relaxing in the warmth.

"You're a Canadian; how can you be cold?" the Sorrentines enquire. They don't understand that while the outdoor temperatures fall far below those of the peninsula, central heating allows us to go sweaterless inside the house. A gas *stufa*, which can only run for short periods and certainly not all night, just can't compare. I can't even heat the bathroom because it is two steps down from the bedroom. The *stufa* has wheels, but it is too heavy to lift.

The shower is a hose hanging from the wall. There is no tub or stall, just a drain in the middle of the floor. Everything gets soaked: toilet, mirror, washing machine. The hot-water heater is the size of a bread box, so I wet my whole body, turn off the water, soap up, rinse quickly. Then I grab a towel from outside the door and sprint up the steps and across the freezing tile floor to dry off in front of the *stufa*. I layer up again: underwear, high-necked sweater, heavy wool sweater, leggings, wool pants, two pairs of socks, shoes.

Along with the winter breeze, flies come in through the various spaces, holes, and cracks. After my shower, I chase them, swatting vigorously in order to warm up. Then, on a good day, I admire my fabulous view before going out. On a bad day, I stay in and consider the room itself.

The only piece of furniture worth looking at is the magnificent wardrobe of shiny dark wood. It stands at least seven feet tall, with six legs, four doors, lots of curves and scrolls on top. My collection of hand-me-downs and cheap German clothes looks pathetic in the cavernous space. My table and chairs are patio plastic, the bed is an army cot, and the dresser is old with drawers that stick. I have put my underwear in the bottom of the wardrobe instead, in an effort to fill it up. A mini fridge is in here, too, while the stove, cupboards, and sink are squeezed into the hallway opposite the bathroom. There is no dryer to go with the washing machine. Dryers are a rarity in southern Italy, and many people don't know they exist. Washing is hung on balcony racks, every day. When it rains, huge sheets of plastic are pegged over the clothes to stop them getting wetter until the sun breaks through.

This is the apartment I rent, but it is not my own private space. There is no lock on the door; the washing machine in my bathroom is used by the rest of the family. The drying rack outside my kitchen window is for their use alone, while I use the one on the balcony off the bedroom. If they run out of gas in their kitchen, they will use my stove. If Mamma has extra food, she leaves a plate for me to find when I come home.

I have no problem with this situation until things start to disappear. Fiorella and Laura begin by borrowing my hair dryer without asking and not returning it. When I go looking for it, they hand it over unapologetically, with no explanation. Then, when I want to refer to my *Let's Go Italy*, I can't find it. I ask Laura, who isn't sure where she put it and then remembers she left it at a friend's house in Positano. She'll try to bring it back soon. I need it now and I'm annoyed, but I hide my irritation; I want to fit in, to make friends, not enemies.

They borrow my CDs, my pots and pans, even my clothes. They never return anything, so I eventually go against principle and resort to ransacking their room, which is adjacent to mine. I will never be sure I have reclaimed all my possessions. Years later, I will wonder whatever happened to my Pink Floyd CD or the grey skirt Ornella gave me, and then in a flash of memory I will suddenly know, without a doubt, exactly where it is.

Laura and Fiorella probably think I'm not bothered at all by their actions. Why should I be? Southern Italy is a land without privacy. Gino, although he wishes for another way of life, has always lived without privacy. His bed is the pull-out couch in the living room; his mother reads his mail and sorts through his things, kept in cupboards throughout the house.

As an only child, I had always believed that what's mine belongs to me alone. I learned how to share with my friends, but I respected their property the way I wanted mine to be respected. I had some idea that siblings didn't always follow the rules, but that was outside my realm. My room was my sanctuary. My closet, my drawers, even the dusty space under the bed was full of secrets. Nothing of any real importance to anyone else, but still *my stuff.* I'm fairly certain that Laura and Fiorella would think nothing of it if I borrowed things from them without asking, but I just can't do it. I don't even want to. I respect the privacy they don't even know they have.

Privacy is just one of the things I miss. Friends and family top the list. But here I have Gino, and I can't bear the thought of leaving. Not for Canada. Certainly not for Australia. As much as I long for home, I want to be here more.

Chapter 15

The second week of February, I arrive home from work to find a telephone message from the police station, stating that my application for a *permesso di soggiorno* has been suspended. I am instructed to appear at the Questura in Naples for a meeting with an officer the following day.

When I tell Gino the name of the officer, he laughs. "That's a stroke of luck! This officer is my brother's friend. I will ask Roberto to speak to him this evening about your situation. I'll meet you tomorrow, and we'll go together."

The officer, Marco, is friendly but serious. He shakes our hands, then indicates for us to take a seat. "The last report I have, dated last week, says that your *richiesta* has been suspended. Unfortunately, the file has been misplaced, and we are unable to locate it at this time." He looks at me, unembarrassed, as if this type of incompetence happens all the time.

"Here's what you need to do: forget about the *permesso di soggiorno*. Instead, you should apply for a work permit. Since you are currently working *al nero*, under the table, this would be in everyone's best interests. Italian law states that since you are not a member of the European Economic Community, you must return to Canada and the Royal School must apply, through the

73

proper legal channels, for your employment. Take note: all *documenti* must be notarized, stamped, and signed, otherwise they are worthless. The school will then courier the *documenti* to you, and you must personally take them to the Italian *consolato* in Canada. There, if everything is in order, they will be stamped and signed again, and you will pay a fee."

I am stuck on the part about returning to Canada. "How long will I have to stay out of Italy?"

"That depends on the *pratica*, but the law requires that you leave Italia for a minimum of three months."

Three months! The Crazy Lady will never hold my position for that long. And she will certainly never spend the time and money to have me come back. There are stacks of résumés from British teachers piling up on her desk. She is even starting to complain about my Canadian accent, which, in the beginning, was so desirable.

Marco's information is confirmed by the Canadian Consulate, which we call from the pay phone outside the Questura.

"Yes," the Canadian official says, "you must have a formal request from an employer in order to work. But if your residency permit comes through, you can renew it each time you exit and reenter the country. Or, you can get married and stay as long as you want."

When I relay this last information to Gino, he smiles at me. "Let's go for pizza and talk it over *con calma*."

At *da Michele*, we hold hands across the table. Gino's eyes penetrate mine, and I know what he's going to say. He takes a breath. "*Allora*, we're probably going to get married one day; why not now?" He squeezes my hands tight in his own, nervous energy passing between us.

Something is not right, and we both feel it. Talking it over, we realize our hearts aren't in it; we don't want Italian bureaucracy dictating when or if we should marry.

"Do you think they would actually throw me out of the country?" I wonder.

"After all, I'm just an English teacher. Wouldn't their time be better spent chasing down thieves or murderers?"

"You're right. Your *pratica* has probably been shoved to the bottom of some drawer in some office. You could go on for years and never hear any more about it. Let's not worry for now."

It is time for me to go to work, so Gino leaves me at the train station. "Remember to sit near the driver," he says, kissing me.

I board the first car, and the doors slide shut, cutting me off from him. The train pulls away from Naples, and I watch the towns and villages roll past.

It is still winter, yet every garden bursts with vegetables. This is the time of year when the fertile slopes of Vesuvius yield rapini, fennel, and lettuces. Trees are laden with sumptuous, glowing fruit. Boxes and crates full of lemons, grapefruit, and oranges spill onto the sidewalk from each *fruttivendolo.*

My perspective has shifted. As usual, it suffices to know that something may be taken away for me to really appreciate it. Instead of thieves and drug addicts on the train, I see families, children, lovers. My heart is with Gino in Naples. Even Sorrento is too far from him. How could I go back to Canada alone?

Arriving at work, I find Julio and his wife in agitated conversation. "*Ciao*, Sheila," says Julio.

The Crazy Lady ignores me, continuing her rant. "We absolutely cannot keep her here any longer!"

"Don't worry, Sheila," soothes Julio. "She's upset because the labour inspector is on his way. You just go home, and we'll sort something out, at least temporarily."

Before I go, I quickly give him the story from the Questura, in English, so he can translate later for his raving wife.

I stand outside the school, thinking how ridiculous this situation has become. There must be a solution, a way to take control. There are two other English schools near Sorrento. I have applied at both, but so far no word. They would most certainly be equally reluctant to sponsor me.

When I arrive home, I find a hot meal of *risotto* and fish

waiting for me. There is also a message from Adamo to say that I am invited for lunch tomorrow. Gino will be meeting me in the evening as usual for our weekend in Positano. If not for all this, now would be the perfect time to move on and away. I never had any intention of becoming so involved.

The next day, I am hesitant to open the door of the Royal School in case the labour inspector is there, ready to pounce. Surprisingly, all is calm.

The Crazy Lady smiles at me through her shroud of cigarette smoke. "Sheila, sit down. We must talk."

I take a seat in the chair near her desk. "This is it," I think. "She is letting me go."

"I have spoken with my *commercialista*, who has connections to the highest officers of the Italian Questura. He says the solution to our problem is simple. You must simply work for us as a freelance *consulente*, instead of as a teacher. Of course, you will continue to teach, but your official title will change, and this is all that matters. We will push for your *permesso di soggiorno* to be approved, once the file is located. This visa, plus the *documento del consulente*, will allow you to stay for as long as you like."

The solution sounds too easy, but I agree to meet with her *commercialista*, whatever that is. If the title of *consulente* will keep the police off my back, I have no reason to object.

"Meet me at Stazione Centrale tomorrow morning, and we will go to Sergio's office together," she says.

My head is spinning as I leave the school. Marco and the Canadian consulate have told me one thing; now Sergio, the *commercialista*, is saying something else. I know I should listen to the former, but I am grasping at straws, looking for a loophole that will allow me to stay. Normally, I wouldn't hesitate to trust the voice of my own consulate, but this is southern Italy, where it's all a matter of whom you know. Even the strictest laws will be bent for those with friends in the right places.

When we arrive, Sergio, the *commercialista*, presents me with a two-page typed document to sign. I have trouble reading the complex terminology and am doubtful of its legality since no lawyers or notaries are present, but I sign it to keep peace and to keep my job. The Crazy Lady and Sergio both stamp it, and I willingly pay a fee of two hundred thousand lire when I see that the contract is written for a million per month, two hundred thousand more than I am making now.

"Since you will no longer be *clandestina*, you must apply for a *codice fiscale* and pay taxes," says Sergio.

So I am a consultant who is still really a teacher, and I make one million lire, which is still really eight hundred thousand after taxes. At least I might now have the chance to work and make future plans with no officials breathing down my neck.

I shake hands with Sergio, and he gives me my final instructions: "Once you obtain the *codice fiscale*, present it to the Questura, along with the *documento del consulente*. If your file has been located, everything can be finalized at that time. If the file is still missing, you can ask to open a new one."

I thank him and follow The Crazy Lady out, precious document in hand.

The next Monday, Gino takes the morning off work to take me to the Intendenza di Finanza to get a *codice fiscale*. I fill out forms, present my passport as identification, pay a fee, and watch as a plastic card with my name and a code number on it appears out of a machine. There are no questions about my reasons for obtaining the card; I am going to pay taxes, and that's all that matters to the Intendenza di Finanza. I feel strangely validated by this new piece of identity. I am part of the system now, safe, a number to be counted with all the rest.

"What does a consultant really do?" I ask Gino.

"Well," he says, "The Crazy Lady asks you what you think

of the Method, and you say, 'I think it's a piece of *merda.*' That's what a consultant does." I laugh so hard I cry.

Returning home to Colli, I find Mamma Russo at the door, hovering like a dazed bumblebee. "The *polizia* called, asking all kinds of questions about you! I told them you were an *amica* staying with us, that you don't work, but they are suspicious! They want to see you first thing *domani!*"

The part about me being a friend covers her own tracks as well as mine; she doesn't declare the income she makes from my rent. The last thing I want is to cause trouble for her by bringing the police around. So I go the next morning and speak with the *Maresciallo*'s assistant.

"Your time as a tourist is up. You must leave the country at once."

"But I have an appointment tomorrow at the Questura in Naples!"

The assistant hesitates a moment, then steps into an office, closing the door behind her. I glance at her desk and see my file, now half an inch thick with various documents and reports. Was it here at the Sorrento police station all the time? How can Naples not know what Sorrento is up to, and vice versa?

The assistant returns and dismisses me with a nod and a glare. "Then go. Report back here in three days. If there is no official word regarding a change in your status, you will have forty-eight hours to leave Italia."

This meeting has unnerved me, but I try to remain confident that my new status as *consulente* and my new tax card will be just what I need.

The morning brings dazzling sunshine, cool sea breezes, and a train strike. A sign at the station tells me that trains are running only as far as Pompeii. There will be a bus to cover the rest of the trip. This should mean only a half-hour delay, the ticket agent assures me. When we arrive in Pompeii, there are no buses. All the other passengers, who are used to such inconveniences, stream onto the highway to hitchhike. I just can't do it. I am rooted to the ground by emotions that have suddenly become too heavy to bear.

I wait for the non-existent bus for twenty minutes, willing it to appear from some distant point on the horizon. Men leer at me from cars. Teenagers on motor scooters call out in dialect, obscenities or greetings, I can't tell which.

I trudge into the station to call Gino's house from the pay phone. He will now be at Stazione Centrale, wondering what has happened to me. Tears of anger, disappointment, and frustration well in my eyes as I try to explain to Gino's mother what has happened. She assures me that Roberto will meet up with Gino at the station and let him know that I am not coming. I take the return train home and cry for hours.

Gino calls and says that he has made another appointment for the following day.

"Don't worry, *tesoro mio*. Be strong. Everything will work out."

I hold his voice in my head all night.

The next morning, Gino and I sit across from the most arrogant, unhelpful man in a uniform I have ever met. "Why are you here?" he barks. "You already know that you must leave or marry. What's it going to be?"

Gino, unconvinced of the legality of Sergio's contract, questions warily, "What if Sheila found work as a consultant? Could she stay?"

"Absolutely not! Consulting work is highly suspect! Holding a *contratto* is reason for expulsion in itself!"

Trembling, I clutch my bag, which contains the contract and the *codice fiscale*. I grip Gino for support.

He shows no outward sign of concern, but I feel the tension in his body. Bargaining is in his blood, and he will not give up easily. He is polite and direct. "We understand that our only current choice is to marry. We would like to request a one-month extension in order to consider such a serious undertaking."

The officer, a true bargainer himself, replies without missing a beat. "You may have until March 1 to think it over."

"But that's only two weeks!" I blurt out.

"It's better than two days. Now go and decide." He deals his final blow as we leave the room: "Remember," he shouts, "even if you do get married, Signorina Wright will not be able to work until she becomes *una citadina italiana*. That process takes three to four years."

Gino leads me to a bench outside the Questura.

"Let's start thinking about moving to Canada instead," he suggests, sadness and seriousness in his eyes. "It can't be this bad. We'll get married. I'll be able to work, *vero*?"

"I have no idea what the immigration laws are in Canada. I've never dealt with a situation like this. I can't even think straight right now."

"Sheila, *amore mio*, let's believe in our *destino*. We were brought together for a reason that magical day by the sea. We are two special people who want to be together. Why should it be so *complicato*?"

I am afraid. This life that I stumbled into is taking over and falling apart at the same time. And I refuse to be pushed into marriage. Not here, not in Canada. And if I stay, married or not, could I survive three or four more years of *al nero* work? Could I withstand the corruption, the crime, the low standard of living? What about raising a family? I'm fairly certain that Gino would be able to work in Canada if he were my husband. But what would he do? He is a glove maker. He adores Italy. No relationship can withstand the distress of an uprooted and unhappy spouse.

My thoughts exhaust me, and I slump on the bench while Gino calls The Crazy Lady. He tells her the whole story, including where she can put her phony contract. There is shouting on both ends, but by the time they both calm down, it has been decided that The Crazy Lady and Sergio will accompany me to the Questura again, to present my case as a contract worker.

"The Crazy Lady thinks Sergio will be able to sort things out," Gino says, no conviction in his voice.

I start to laugh. At this point, I have nothing to lose. I will expect nothing more than the satisfying sound of The Crazy Lady admitting she was wrong. If she and Sergio want to waste more time on this ridiculous caper, then let them.

Gino starts to laugh, too. "Come here, *amore*," he says, kissing me. "Next weekend we will go away somewhere romantic and forget this whole mess."

The next morning, I report to the police station in Sorrento as requested. The *Maresciallo* glares at me when I tell him of the two-week extension. "Where's the receipt?" he barks.

"They didn't give me one."

He pulls a sheet out of my enormous file. "It says here you must leave. I'll have to report you immediately."

Before he has the chance to fill out more forms regarding my illicit activities, I point to the phone. "Please just call the Questura. They will vouch for me," I say, not at all sure that they will.

Miraculously, he calls. Even more miraculously, there is an officer on the other end who knows what is going on. He verifies my story and confirms the two-week extension.

"What do you think you can accomplish in two weeks?" the *Maresciallo* sneers.

I am silent, tired of this game. But then, since I have someone of authority in front of me, I ask a question: "If I marry, how long will it be before I can work?"

"Right away, of course. As soon as you are *sposata*, you can do whatever you like."

"*Grazie*." I leave, screaming inside with frustration.

Later, on the phone with Gino, I let myself rant: "Is this just the word of an ignorant policeman, or does he really know something the officer in Naples didn't? Why can't I get a straight answer on anything?"

Gino is calm, as usual. "Sheila, you must understand something: no Italian official will allow himself to admit he doesn't know. He will *inventare* an answer rather than appear unknowledgeable."

"So how will I ever find out the right answer?"

"There can be any number of right answers in Italia, depending on the *situazione*."

"I can't live like this! Tomorrow is Valentine's Day, and I get to spend it at the Questura with The Crazy Lady and her shifty *commercialista*. I don't want to waste my last two weeks here playing stupid mind games with Italian officials!"

"I don't have much *fiducia* in Sergio, either," Gino says, "but if there is still a small chance that things will work out, don't you think it's worth a try? Think of it as part of the *avventura*."

"I want my adventure to be sun, sea, and romance," I whine.

"You'll have that, too. Be strong, have *pazienza*. Give it one last try."

"Okay," I sigh.

I want him to stop telling me to be strong and patient. I want him to whisk me away to someplace where none of this is happening, where just the two of us exist and nothing else matters.

At the station the next morning, I find that the nine o'clock train has been cancelled. I wait twenty minutes for the next train, which arrives on time. I breathe a sigh of relief as we move away from the platform. I should still be able to make the appointment.

Four stops out, an announcement comes over the loudspeaker: "Due to occupation of the Torre Annunziata station, this train will stop at Pompeii." Even more annoying than strikes, occupation of a station or tracks can happen at any time, with no warning. The numerous unemployed in southern Italy consider it an effective way of making a statement. Normally, I might sympathize with their plight, but this is more than I can take.

I think about Gino and how he would react in this situation. He would probably take it all in stride, as most southerners do. And so I resign myself. If there is a bus at Pompeii, I will take it. If there isn't, I'll simply go home. Gino is at work today, so he won't be left waiting at the station. Knowing that he will not be worried helps to ease my mind. I have little hope for this appointment. Missing it will certainly not be the end of the world.

At Pompeii, I call Julio and The Crazy Lady to warn them of the delay, then I follow the rest of the passengers onto a bus. It is a regular city bus, not intended to hold a trainload of people. We cram ourselves in. I stand, squeezed against a sweaty man whose breath tickles my neck and a short teenage boy whose greasy hair rubs a dark stain into my sleeve. Being a city bus, it makes all the usual stops. This routine is useless, as no one intends to get off before the next train station, and certainly no one else can board. At one stop, a conductor pushes into the crowd and asks to see our tickets. When he tries to throw off some teenagers who haven't paid, a fight breaks out; by the time the boys get off, the conductor is bleeding from several gashes on his face.

I am disgusted and sad, but I have no choice but to persevere. I try to imagine these towns the way they used to be. Gino has told me that the royalty of Europe came here for holidays, that majestic villas once lined the coast, that it was called *Il Miglio d'Oro*, The Golden Mile, for its elegance and exclusiveness. Now it is the land of drug lords. Along the broken streets we travel, nothing remains of the former glory.

We circumnavigate Torre Annunziata and arrive at Leopardi to find a train waiting. I board along with the rest of the passengers, many of whom are now grumbling about the delay. I no longer care about the appointment, which I have surely missed. My only desire is to see Gino. I walk from the train station to the factory, following the route Gino and I took when we visited his family. I am numb, hardly noticing the traffic, smells, and grime.

The factory door is open, and I can see Gino working at the huge *pressa*. He catches sight of me and smiles, as if this is the most normal place to meet me. I describe my ordeal while Gino holds me in his arms, and his brothers try to cheer me up.

"We can easily fix up another appointment for tomorrow," says Roberto.

I am focused more on my growing dislike of Italy. How has my life come to this? Why am I spending my Saturdays at the Questura or on buses and trains trying to get there? It cuts especially deep because I know I am responsible. I *am* here illegally. I *am* working illegally. What did I expect?

Sergio is unperturbed when I call to apologize for standing him up. "*Nessun problemo*," he says. "Meet me at ten o'clock tomorrow."

I spend the night at Gino's place. His mother fusses and fishes for information. "You *povera* girl…. When will you be leaving Italia?" She makes up Gino's bed for us, a situation so awkward, I can hardly watch, let alone help.

Gino takes me into the kitchen. "I told my mother that if I wanted to sleep with you for reasons other than just sleeping, I certainly wouldn't do it at *her* house."

This rationale doesn't make me feel much better.

We rise early in the morning. Gino's mother is already up, making coffee. She clears her throat nervously before tapping lightly on the door.

"*Il caffè è pronto.*"

Gino takes yet another morning off work. We meet Sergio as arranged, then wait for over an hour to see an official. "This man is *molto importante*," says Sergio. "He will give us the straight story."

Sergio's contact has yet another answer for us: "Yes, the *signorina* must leave Italia, but as for the *contratto*, she can have it approved and stamped at the Italian embassy in Canada and then return immediately."

"What if we fax the *documento* to the embassy and have it approved that way?" asks Sergio.

"You can try that. As it stands now, the *contratto* is worthless."

"*Allora*, well then, we'll simply call the embassy," says Sergio haughtily, obviously embarrassed by the invalidity of his two-hundred-thousand-lire contract.

We return together to the Royal School, where The Crazy Lady herself calls the embassy. She speaks to several officials while I wait on the edge of my chair. When she hangs up, real regret in her eyes, I know it's over.

"*Mi dispiace*, Sheila. I'm sorry. There is nothing we can do. The processing time would be six months, and an inspector would have to come to the school. The situation is simply *impossibile*. I really am sorry." She kisses me.

Julio shakes Gino's hand, then mine. "I wish it could have worked out, Sheila. The students will miss you."

We leave the Royal School for the last time. Outside, I am thankful Gino is there to help me put my emotions in order. I have no job, and only two weeks left in Italy. I feel defeated, but at the same time, now that certain lines have been defined, I see the glimmer of a fresh start emerge.

"Gino, you know how much I miss my family. Perhaps some time at home would be good for me. I know three months is a long time, but you could come and visit over the Easter holidays. I can come back in June as a tourist; we can get a place together and then decide about marriage."

These thoughts are not new. We have been talking over our options for weeks. The difference now is that some choices have been removed.

"You could still go to Australia for a while if you want," says Gino.

"Australia is the farthest thing from my mind these days. I

just want to be with you. If I can't do that, then I want to go home, where I can find some sort of job to finance the trip and allow me to contribute to our life together when I get back."

"You don't have to worry about money. I will support us."

We both know the rents on the peninsula are exorbitant and that Gino's salary rises and falls with the seasons. I hug him. He is the most generous person I have ever met.

"Do you think we will be able to find an apartment before I leave?"

"*Possiamo provare*, we can try, but if we don't, you can be sure I will spend every weekend looking for one while you are away. My *famiglia* has promised to help us any way they can, financially or otherwise."

One important positive outcome of this adventure is that Gino's relationship with his family has undergone a huge change for the better. Underneath his previous antipathy towards his parents, a profound love and respect has been exposed. His brothers especially have rallied to support us, covering for him at work, offering assistance of all kinds, and accepting me wholeheartedly. They all work together every day of the week, arguing over a new style or print, cursing Roberto for arriving late, Gennaro for leaving early, but when it comes to what's really important, they are there for each other.

Roberto, always the one with contacts, knows someone at a travel agency. Through him, Gino books me a flight for March 1. I wonder if Canadian winter will have relented by then. Snow and ice storms can last until April, so I have little hope.

The end so near in sight, I have no trouble appreciating once again, with an added touch of melancholy, the charms of the peninsula. Bougainvillea blooms madly along the sunny Amalfi Coast. Tissue-thin flowers of purple, magenta, and red entwine themselves around whitewashed arches, grey stone walls, and terra-cotta terraces.

No longer tied to the schedule of the Royal School, I take solo day trips to Ravello, Amalfi, and Positano. Some days I am tempted to swim, but the frigid February sea discourages me. I visit with Adamo, who insists I take two bottles of homemade wine to my father.

"Your father appreciates wine, no? He surely deserves at least one white and one red from my *cantina*."

Adamo's wine is an acquired taste. Too close a cousin of vinegar, it is one thing to sip it by the sea as a light but potent chaser to sweet, fleshy chestnuts. It would be another thing altogether to smuggle it past Canada Customs, only to have my father gag on his steak and potatoes at the sight of large chunks of sediment floating in his glass. I take the bottles, but they never make it into my suitcase.

I call home to let my parents in on the new development. They are so far away in every sense. Not wanting to worry them, I have not kept them entirely up to date. Now they misunderstand my imminent return. They are too sympathetic in a you-had-an-adventure-now-it's-time-to-come-home sort of way.

There is so much inside me that I just can't say into the telephone.

Chapter 16

We have no car to access the mountain villages, so we search for an apartment along the train route in Sorrento, Sant'Agnello, Piano, and Meta. The places we see are small and damp, mostly renovated *cantine* with noisy street-level windows and low ceilings. We could probably find an apartment in Naples, but Gino insists we should stay on the peninsula, even if it means he will have to travel two hours a day on the train. My faith in Gino's capabilities keeps me from becoming discouraged.

"I'm sure I'll find something while you're away," he assures me.

I believe him. This is one of those times when I have to let go.

Lisa, my replacement, is at the Royal School when I pick up my last pay.

She is finished for the day, so we walk to the bus stop together. She pronounces "bus" as "boose" and I smile to myself, imagining her students all speaking with a Yorkshire accent.

She is in no hurry to go home; her apartment is a dark hole-in-the-wall on a noisy street, and her boyfriend is working long hours as a tour guide. We decide to go for gelato and immediately strike up a friendship in the manner of solo women abroad. We tell each other condensed but intimate details about our lives.

"You are lucky that your future mother-in-law is thirty miles away in Naples," she says. "Dario lives in Sorrento with his mother and aunt. They drive me batty with their constant criticism and insinuations. They expect me to cook, clean, and do laundry all day. They won't let him move into my apartment because he's the only child and both the crabby old battle-axes need looking after. Take my advice: move to Canada with Gino and never come back to this godforsaken backward country!"

I have to laugh at her, because in the next breath she tells me how we should spend the following day sunning on the beach in Positano.

"There's nowhere like it," she sighs. "Except for all those bloody steps, it's paradise on Earth. We could go to that fabulous *alimentari* near the church; they make the best mozzarella and artichoke *panini*. Then we could take the bus up to Ravello and have cappuccino on the terrace. What do you say?"

I say yes. I have no plans until the weekend.

On Saturday, Gino and I take the slow boat to Capri. There are only seventy-two hours left before my plane leaves for Canada, but we will not be rushed. We will spend this day, my twenty-ninth birthday, savouring the island and each other. We will even spend the night on Capri, in a hotel, a luxury we surely deserve, but first, we will relish the journey. I am excited to see the peninsula from a different angle.

"There's Adamo's terrace!" I shout, pointing high up the cliff to where a wooden railing is just visible among the lemon trees. We can't see the house, situated on the other side of the grove. The terrace is an entity unto itself, built solely for delight. What could be more relaxing after a morning of labour under the trees than to put one's feet up against the Mediterranean in the shade of lemons?

Outsiders now, we pass the archway that leads to Queen Giovanna's baths. Our wake rocks gently through, exposing for a moment the ruins that lie beneath the surface. Then there is the cape itself, completely void today of tourists, though the end of February brings a hint of spring and we sit comfortably on deck in light jackets. Our eyes are drawn to the rock where we met almost four months ago. So much has happened since then, it seems as if we have already been together for at least a year.

"We have come a long way in a short time," says Gino, his thoughts echoing mine. He takes my hand in one of his, and with the other pulls a small parcel out of his pocket. It is store-wrapped in the Italian custom. Shiny green paper shows the gold embossed insignia of a jewellery store. There is a gold ribbon, too, tied and curled by expert hands. "*Buon compleanno,*" he says.

I take the gift and open it carefully, not wanting the wind to carry away the paper or the box and what might lie inside. I lift the lid of the box to find a ring made of swirls of gold. Eight tiny diamonds adorn the swirls, which meet at an emerald centre.

Gino stops me as I move to try it on. "Emerald is not your birthstone, but the *bellezza* of this ring made me think of you. There is an inscription, too."

There are five letters engraved on the inside of the ring: YAH-MH. I am puzzled for a moment, but then Gino puts my hand on his chest and tells me what they mean: "You Are Holding My Heart"—a line from the first movie we had seen together. It had been in English with Italian subtitles, so we were both able to enjoy it. Sharing something as simple as that had meant a lot to us, given our daily struggle to communicate.

Crushing the ring into my palm so tightly it leaves an imprint, I throw my arms around Gino and squeeze my eyes shut in order to preserve this moment in my memory. We separate, but I remain pressed against his side, my head on his shoulder as I try the ring on, placing it on the middle finger of my right hand, where it rests perfectly, glowing against my skin. It seems to absorb the sun rather than reflect it, so that I may carry warmth wherever I go.

We walk up to Capri town from the port, rather than taking the *funicolare*. Steep, narrow alleyways and countless steps lead us past private gardens and courtyards bursting with roses and bougainvillea. Twenty minutes later, the centre *piazza* welcomes us with wrought-iron benches and a splendid view over the Gulf.

Other tourists share our bliss, for Capri is an international dream destination, any time of year. A hydrofoil pulls into port, its giant steel wings relaxing into a resting position. Still more visitors disembark and line up for the *funicolare*. In the summer, hundreds of boats, both public and private, come and go in a constant relay race from Sorrento, Naples, and other ports along the coast. The square is standing room only during *la stagione*. Many tour guides, restaurateurs, and shop owners make so much money during the summer months they can take the winter off. Businesses cut back on hours, some close, but Capri is never deserted.

Gino and I are truly on holiday. The boat has carried us that much farther away from our troubles. We have escaped momentarily and can admire Naples far across the bay as the other visitors do. For the next twenty-four hours, we will simply lose ourselves on Capri.

Our room at the Stella Maris is small but adequate. We leave our bags and make our first excursion to the gardens of Augustus, following winding cobbled streets to the other side of the island. In the gardens, flowering plants mixed with thick vines and succulent *agave* line the walkways and terraces. We lean against the sun-warmed railing and gaze down the cliff and out to sea where the *Faraglioni* lie. An archway in the middle of one of these monstrous rocks allows small boats to pass through. Seagulls whirl above the cliffs until they spot a fishing boat heading for port.

As we walk up to a higher terrace, I marvel at the *agave* and other exotic vegetation. Gino explains that the *Scirocco*, the warm wind from Africa, brings not only sand, but also tiny seeds that find Capri the first resting place in their voyage across the Mediterranean. We sit for a few minutes on a bench and peruse our map from the tourist office. It shows a trail right around this end of the island.

"Let's try it," says Gino. "We'll find a place to have our picnic, and then when we've finished the hike, we can take the bus over to Anacapri."

Anacapri is the only other town on the island. Farther from the port than Capri town, buses make the trip every few minutes. It is the place to start if you want to visit the famous Blue Grotto or if you want to take a cable car to the top of Monte Solaro. There is also a renowned mosaic on the floor of the church of San Michele, the Villa of Axel Munthe, and plenty of shops and restaurants.

Following the map, we reach a steep path leading down towards the sea. It is clearly a detour from the main trail, but we take it, drawn as we always are by the sound of waves on rock. The sea has become rough in the last hour, and I'm glad we took the early boat. The *Maestrale* wind is punctual, whipping up the water every afternoon, sometimes into millions of sparkling ripples that nibble playfully at the shore. Other times it works the sea into a frenzy of whitecaps that beat furiously against one another and any object that falls in their path.

We descend to the rhythmic booming of large waves. The steps bring us to a concrete platform built into the rocks, almost at sea level. The owners of the hotel above have taken advantage of this naturally sheltered spot to construct a *lido*, a man-made beach where clients can sunbathe on *lettini* and swim in the lagoon formed by chunks of cliff that must have separated themselves from the mainland many years before. The sea leaps towards us, thwarted by the barrier. Spray is in our faces, and Gino searches for the perfect photo location.

"Stand there in front of the waves," he says.

I notice that while the sea is hurling itself against the natural breakwater, only drops like light rain reach this side. I position myself.

"Here comes a big one," Gino says, finger on the shutter release. I smile broadly. A rumble like a subway train passing far below resonates through my feet and up into my chest. I turn to look and before the shriek has escaped my throat, I am drenched. I run to Gino, drops of seawater flying from my hair. He sweeps me up, and we laugh like children, clutching each other, and I don't know if the salt I taste is from my tears or the sea. Two elderly fishermen watch us from the shade of the cliff.

"*Salve*," says Gino, suddenly all serious, then we collapse into laughter again. Gino gives me his jacket, draping mine across his backpack to dry in the sun. I shake out my hair.

"Let me take one more picture of you looking like a *bella sirena*," he says.

I pose again, safely cliffside this time, to the amusement of the fishermen.

"Let's find a place to eat our picnic," I say. "I'm starving."

"Me, too." Gino leads the way back up the steps to the trail.

In Italy, there is almost always a bench just where you need it. This one must belong to the hotel on the cliff. From where we sit, we can look straight down onto the scene of my drenching. The *Maestrale* is relentless, but the sun is warm in this sheltered, south-facing spot. Gino opens his pack and sets out our *pranzo* between us on the bench: tuna and tomato sandwiches prepared at the *salumeria* across from the hotel, great round slices of *provolone*, and a bottle of red wine.

At no time today have we been more than two miles from the town of Capri, but we have been first to one side of the island and then the other, down to the sea and up again, and with a full afternoon and evening ahead of us, we fall on the spread, devouring every last crumb and exclaiming over the exquisiteness of each bite.

Gino stretches and sighs. "Ah, if every day could be like this...."

I nod in agreement, but what I know is this: that the dreadfully low moments make the high ones seem higher, that we would perhaps scarcely recognize joy if there were no sadness in our lives. Certainly my own perception of this moment is paradoxically coloured in rainbows by the sombre shadow of my impending departure.

We are torn between wanting to stay seated in the sun for hours and a desire to see as much of the island as possible during our short stay. We compromise. Half an hour more on the bench, then we heave ourselves into action. The rest of the trail follows the cliff around the end of the island, dense brush on one side, Mediterranean on the other.

Close to the end, just before the trail becomes alleyways and cobbled streets leading back into town, we encounter two remarkable natural phenomena. The first, located at the base of a steep stairway, is the Grotta di Matermania, a large cave facing the sea that was once a Roman sanctuary. And then, breathless with discovery and the effort of climbing a hundred steps through undergrowth and vines, we emerge in front of the Arco Naturale, a giant rock arch that reaches out towards Punta Campanella on the mainland, reminiscent of the time when Capri was not yet an island.

On our way back to town, we stop for gelato at a bar. Mine is a mix of *nocciola*, hazelnut, and *stracciatella*, chocolate chip. We walk on, digging into our *coppe* with tiny plastic spoons, savouring every bite. Reenergized now, we head for the hotel to freshen up before taking the bus to Anacapri. Freshening up, however, turns into more; as I step out of the shower, Gino pulls me down onto the bed and covers me with kisses.

Often, hotel beds are two lumpy, saggy singles joined together, and the large fissure down the middle, known to us as *la grotta*, can be immensely annoying for couples who wish to sleep close but not crushed into each other. These mattresses are pleasantly futon-firm, however, and we eventually drift into a relaxed slumber.

We awaken to the sound of music and many voices. It is late afternoon, and we are hungry again. Instead of making the trek over to Anacapri, we walk to the square to see what all the noise is. In our self-absorbed state, we had forgotten that it is *Carnevale*, the Italian version of Mardi Gras. The square is full of costumed revellers, dancing the *Tarantella* or eating pizza at one of the many restaurants that flank the square. There are colourful *arlecchini*, *baute* in three-cornered hats, and sequined *pulcinelle* in tulle and lace.

The beat of the party has drawn us in, but what we really want is to be alone together. We order sandwiches and wine at the *salumeria* and walk out to the Arco Naturale. We can't see it in the dark, but its presence is palpable. The sea air comes cool through the pines, but the wind has dropped and we are comfortable on a stone bench, still slightly warm from the sun. We eat and drink, then return to the hotel to make love again. Anacapri can wait.

Chapter 17

When my day of departure comes, Mamma Russo walks me to the bus stop. For once, I am glad to see a cloud encasing Colli di Fontanelle. The heavy opaqueness fits my mood. Mamma kisses me and bids me *buon viaggio* as the orange bus pulls into the square. The driver asks me where I'm going, but I know he already knows.

I am big news in the village. All eyes are on me and my new backpack, recently purchased in Naples. The scarf-clad shopping ladies, normally so reticent, nod and smile in my direction. Are they sorry to see me go? Or are they glad to be rid of the foreigner with the police record? One thing they are not is indifferent. They will talk about me long after I'm gone.

We wind down out of the mountain clouds to sunny Sant'Agnello, where bougainvillea blooms and palm trees sway in the Mediterranean breeze. Here, spring laughs gaily in my face as I voyage reluctantly toward winter. This is the wrong kind of travel, the kind that pushes against the will of the spirit. To stop is one thing, but to be dragged by the heels back to where you started is just plain heartbreaking.

Gino meets me at Stazione Centrale in Naples. I remember the first time he met me here, how my nerves tingled in anticipation. Now he is here to help me depart, for three months, this life we have made. We board the airport bus outside the station. It leaves a wake of acrid exhaust as we roar and rumble over cobbled streets to Capodichino airport. We hold hands as usual, but there is little to say. Anything we might express is far too intimate for this crowded environment.

After I check in, we buy cappuccinos and *cornetti* and sit by a window overlooking the runway. I focus on the positive, on the new adventures that await us. "It will only be six weeks until you come for Easter. I can't wait to show you where I come from and to have you meet my parents."

"I will think of you every day and dream of you every night," says Gino, brown eyes shining with sincerity.

In Canada, six weeks pass in a flurry of part-time jobs, dinners by the fire with my parents, and visits with friends where I laugh until I cry at their comprehensible humour. They wonder briefly why Italy has turned me into the village idiot, but what they really want to know is my story. My parents are surprised when I tell them I have a return ticket to Italy, and subsequently not so surprised to hear that Gino will be visiting at Easter. They are prepared to maintain their usual cautious-but-open-minded stance.

The instant Gino steps through the door, my parents are swept up in his aura of charm and strength. He brings them wine and lemon liqueur, even a torpedo-sized *provolone* and jumbo jar of sun-dried tomatoes. I smile to see they are astounded by his appetite, as I knew they would be. They are endlessly interested in his family, his work, his country. I wonder if they realize how serious our relationship is. They must see it in our eyes.

Gino and I drive to Algonquin Park, where I introduce him to Canadian nature: moose at the roadside, four-foot-high beaver dams, and loon song by tranquil lakes. It is mid-April, but Gino's winter jacket from Naples isn't warm enough here. There is still some snow on the ground and ice on the forest trails. Gino is Bambi; his legs have no sense of ice; they simply fly out from under him, leaving both his behind and his dignity bruised.

April outdoors might be biting winds and icy paths, but indoors it is fire-glow and all-encompassing warmth. We relax by the hearth in the evenings, just as I had imagined, listening to my father's classical CDs. There is no sound from outside, save the odd bark of a nearby farm dog.

We stay a night in Toronto. Gino is thrilled to stay in a motel. "It's just like in the American films!" he enthuses.

He loves the anonymity of it. I love his perspective. I am seeing my country through his eyes, and it is fascinating. I had never given much thought to how free of trash and grime Canadian cities are. Or how obeying traffic lights makes so much sense.

Of course, there are things Gino misses. He finds the coffee so unpalatable, even in specialty cafés, that he resorts to drinking hot chocolate at breakfast. He wonders at the tasteless selection of cheeses available in supermarkets and how anyone can survive without fresh-pressed olive oil. He misses the sea, the kind southern climate, and *piazza*s full of families.

After he leaves, I wait impatiently for Gino's phone calls and letters, and for June 1. In the middle of May, a letter arrives telling me he has rented an apartment in Meta di Sorrento. No details, just that he has been very *fortunato* to find it and he will be interested to see my reaction when I arrive. He sends me infinite *baci* and *abbracci*, kisses and hugs. I replace the letter in its envelope and return to my waiting, with even more impatience.

Part Two

Chapter 18

I am nervous passing through Italian customs, certain that I will be detained and searched at least, or turned away at worst. Miraculously, the officer glances only briefly at the first page of my passport, then slaps it onto the counter and slides it back to me. No questions, no stamps. I'm relieved, but furtive, like a shoplifter who hasn't yet escaped the vicinity.

I catch a glimpse of Gino through the glass. He is summer-handsome already, skin darker, hair slightly lighter, wearing a bright turquoise polo shirt and white jeans. He hasn't spotted me yet, stuck as I am in the crowd with my cart full of suitcases crammed with books, gifts, peanut butter, and maple syrup.

The crowd carries me through the sliding doors and into the waiting area. Gino's arms are around me, and I smell the sun on his skin.

"*Andiamo,*" he says, commandeering my cart. "I have Ettore's car outside."

Letting him take the lead, I feel the tension lift from my shoulders. I follow him out into the blinding sunshine, one step farther from Passport Control. I am almost weightless, buoyed along in his wake of strength and confidence. We reach an old, dusty, white Ibiza *Seat* (pronounced Say-at) and Gino heaves my bags into the trunk.

"Don't mind the dents and dirt," he says. "It's got a great *motore*. Ettore says he'll sell it to us in a few months, once he buys a new one."

Our own car! I hadn't even dared to hope.

"We'll go straight to Meta," he continues. "My family can wait a few days for a visit. I want you all to myself for a while."

His eyes are joyful, mirroring mine. I am back, and we are about to start a life together under the sun, by the sea, in our very own apartment. I hug him. "*Andiamo!*"

I open the window as Gino drives the coastal highway towards our peninsula. Summer has already taken a firm hold here and the breeze is warm. The greenery is even more lush than I remember, the sea more iridescent. Everything is loud: the traffic around us, the wind, the cicadas in the nearby pines. Now I see Capri far out in the bay, and I think of our last trip there. I touch Gino's arm, and he glances my way, pure desire illuminating his face. A strong tingle, almost violent, travels through my body.

Being in the car is freedom. We could go anywhere, on our own schedule. To Vesuvius, shadowing ominously to our left; over the mountains to Salerno, Paestum, or even farther south down the coast to Calabria and eventually to Sicily. Today, however, we are going to set up house in Meta di Sorrento, the first town after the last mountain tunnel, four short train stops before the Sorrento terminus.

I toured Meta once, in Costantino's shiny red Fiat, after dark. Meta is his home town, and he expertly navigated the narrow cobbled streets, fearlessly downshifting into alleyways where I held my breath, waiting for the scrape of my door on the too-close walls. Then he would speed up again, across a square, dodging sleeping dogs, to dive once again into another *vicoletto* where, had we stopped midway through, neither one of us would have been able to open our doors.

Now, in the bright light of day, I am unable to recognize any of those squares, streets, or *vicoletti*. Gino drives cautiously, having been a patron of public transportation for most of his life. The streets, intended centuries ago for foot and donkey travel, allow only one-way traffic. We must back into gateways while more aggressive drivers pass. Gino honks the horn at each intersection; there are no traffic lights or stop signs, and visibility is minimal, like being inside a labyrinth.

We reach the main square, tiny really, but seemingly a huge open space at the centre of the maze. Gino coaxes the car into the only available parking spot, next to an overflowing dumpster. I have to climb over the stick shift to exit on Gino's side. The air is ripe with the stench of rotting garbage.

"There has been a *sciopero,* strike, for a week," Gino says. "The garbage is usually picked up nightly." Stray dogs hang around, attracted by the smell, but they pay no attention to us. We start to haul my bags out of the trunk. "Don't bother with the heavy stuff," Gino says. "I'll come back for it in *un minuto.*"

Our apartment is located in the building behind the wall where we parked, a convent built in the 1600s, converted years ago into a rabbit warren of dwellings. We pass a huge iron gate that leads to an arched doorway under what once must have been a bell tower. "That's an entrance to our place," says Gino. "But the landlord has blocked off the lower part of the apartment, so we have to enter from another door."

We turn up a steep *vicoletto*, and I laugh in amazement as Gino demonstrates the narrowness of the street by reaching out and touching both sides at once. Small cars do pass here, however, as the scraped and paint-scarred walls attest. We walk to the first door on the right. It is heavy oak, painted dark green, with a brass knocker in the shape of a fist. One step up from the street, the doorway is just deep enough for us to squeeze into as a car the size of Topolino toils past.

Gino takes out a key worthy of a castle and opens our door. We are not in the apartment, but rather in a sunny cloister. There are whitewashed arches and flowering vines and plants in terra-cotta pots, and at the opposite end, a tall iron gate through which I glimpse a garden full of fruit trees. Two sets of stone stairs lead up from this cloister-courtyard to apartments above, but our door is near the garden gate, a modern entrance this time of heavy glass and metal shutters.

Gino opens this door with a much smaller key, and we enter our home. It is cool and dim in contrast to the brightness outside. A window lets in light from the garden, and I gaze in wonder at this massive expanse of tile and marble that is to be my kitchen, the place where I will cook and eat and greet my lover as he returns from work.

There is a wood-burning pizza oven in one corner, a marble table and matching counters, cupboards with sliding doors that reach up to the whitewashed vaulted ceiling, a small washing machine, fridge, and gas stove. The floor is spotless white tile, which I love on impulse but will later curse as it shamelessly flaunts every footprint, crumb, and coffee drip. Sweeping alone will never appease this demanding floor, and I will end up mopping it daily, after stacking the white iron chairs on the table as all Italian *casalinghe* do.

I'll enjoy cooking on the gas stove, where hot is hot when you need it and off is off, no messing around. I imagine the pizza parties we will have with our friends, the meals we will share with visitors from home, English lessons I will teach while sipping espresso made in my very own *moka*. And this is just the first room. Overwhelmed, I hug Gino.

"It's very *economico*, but there are a few conditions," he says. "The landlord has relatives who come in the summer, so we will have to vacate the premises for the month of *agosto* each year. And we won't have access to the full apartment, only the upper portion where we are now."

Gino leads me out of the kitchen to a room that will come to be known as *lo studio*, the study, really just an all-purpose area between the kitchen and bedroom. He shows me some terra-cotta stairs leading down to an arched doorway, completely blocked by a large slab of wood.

There is a tiny crack in the wood, however, and I take the ten steps down to press my face against it. I can tell only that the room below seems to be enormous, although I can't be sure of the true dimensions, my vision being so restricted. The only light comes from a glass door at the far end. There is enough illumination to see that the walls are white like the rest of the apartment, but the floor is tiled in terra-cotta instead of the shiny white tiles upstairs. Various cabinets with glass doors line the walls, but I can't tell what's inside them. A monstrous oak dining table with chairs dominates the centre of the room.

There seems to be a mountain of boxes, beds, and various miscellaneous items piled against the slab of wood where I now lean. It certainly doesn't budge with my weight. I climb back to the top of the stairs where Gino waits.

"We'll have everything we need up here," he says. "For the price, we certainly can't demand more."

The study has a table and chairs, a wall unit with shelves and cupboards, and a single bed. French doors with thick wooden shutters face onto the cloister-courtyard. Next is the bedroom. About the same size as the study, it has matching French doors, a chest of drawers, a mammoth *armadio*, and two single beds pushed together to make our *matrimoniale*. I look at the bed and sigh. It seems we can't escape *la grotta*.

At the far end of the bedroom is a small hallway with a closet on one side and a bathroom on the other. The bathroom houses a toilet, sink, and bidet. No tub, no shower stall. Just a showerhead on the wall and a drain in the middle of the floor. I sigh again, but my enthusiasm will not be quashed.

We walk back to the kitchen, and I realize that all the rooms are in a row along the courtyard, with the bathroom closest to the green entrance door and the kitchen backing onto the inner garden. If we are in the kitchen and want to reach the bathroom, we have to go through the study and the bedroom. "Not the best if we have guests to stay," I remark.

"I'm sure we'll manage," says Gino, ever the optimist. "Any guests of ours will be sure to fit in."

He's right, and I am still too thrilled by the kitchen and courtyard to spend time worrying about a minor inconvenience. I don't even notice the lack of a living room, heating devices, or comfortable furniture.

We step out into the courtyard, where Gino opens the garden gate with another key. "The landlord will be here from time to time to tend his vegetables. He said we can have a corner to grow herbs if we want."

This garden is an unexpected bonus. Southern Italian towns are so densely populated that space is a valuable commodity. People lucky enough to have gardens utilize every inch, and a bargain apartment is usually just someone's converted basement *cantina*. Here, we are blessed with a patio area complete with marble table. We picture ourselves eating many *al fresco* meals, surrounded by walnut, fig, orange, and lemon trees, the Meta mountain our backdrop.

"Shall we go and unpack your things?" asks Gino.

"Absolutely," I say, as we turn back and step into our home.

Chapter 19

The Monday after we move in, Gino must rise at six o'clock in order to catch the 6:25 train to Naples so he can be at the factory by eight o'clock. The bed, which caves softly towards the centre, tries to pull him back. Buried in my own pocket of *la grotta*, I manage only to utter a muffled "*Ciao, amore*" before resuming my dreams.

He will eat breakfast at the factory: a small carton of milk bought along the way, to which he adds espresso and chestnut honey (to the disgust of his brothers), and a package of *plum cakes*, mini square muffins, like pound cake but not quite as dense. Once I figure out the stove and oven, I will begin experimenting with cakes and *biscotti* myself.

Gino readies himself silently; I register only his gentle kiss and the final click of the latch on the door.

It is nine o'clock by the time I wake fully to my first day alone in Meta. The bedroom is still dark; the solid shutters keep out all but a sliver of light. I instantly sense Gino's absence in the pit of my stomach, an almost grieflike loss that immobilizes me. I try to focus on the excitement of having a day to myself to explore, to organize my new house. I remind myself how much I treasure time alone, how my life as an only child has taught me to be self-reliant, even often wishing to be left to my own devices when in the company of others.

I make my way to the kitchen and peek out the window into the garden, where a cloudless sky frames the lemon tree. My spirit starts to rise, aided by the aroma of espresso, which is soon bubbling vigorously in the *moka*. I sit down with my *caffè latte* and two chocolate cookies, a breakfast I would never have allowed myself in Canada.

I turn on the radio, rolling the dial aimlessly. I can't follow the news. The rapid language bombards me. By the time I've deciphered one sentence topic, I've missed the next three. There is music, too. Incomprehensible lyrics flow into each other, making me feel suddenly irritable, as if there is just too damn much foreignness in my life.

I want to hear English, to know what is going on around me, not to be mired in constant confusion. Even Gino and I have never had a real conversation, at least not one like I have with other native English speakers—one where you don't have to pick and choose every word, where you laugh easily at subtle jokes, where it all flows naturally, without effort.

It is easy to speak Italian one on one with Gino. He is patient and speaks clearly. I know he wants to learn English, but I need to fit in so badly, I take all the learning for myself. I keep notes, thrilled by new expressions and delicious words like *chiarezza*, clarity, and *scoperta*, discovery. There is never a lull in the conversation, since the language itself is subject to discussion. After a while, I notice that we are speaking only in Italian unless Gino requests an English lesson, and it feels almost natural.

Outside our insular, romantic nucleus, things are different. In Naples, I listen to Gino and his brothers banter in dialect over lunch, and I'm back in the black hole of incomprehension. They laugh loudly, boisterously, and I want desperately to climb up out of the hole into their world.

It is rare for me to laugh here, really laugh, freely and spontaneously, so that the tears come to my eyes. I am hesitant, not sure I have understood the joke, not wanting to expose myself as a fool, always left behind.

In order to function fully here, I would need to know three languages: Italian, Neapolitan, and Gesture. How have I lived my whole life with such a poor vocabulary of body language? I consider myself daring if I raise my middle finger to say "screw you." Neapolitan gestures are much more complex—sometimes subtle, sometimes vulgar, often combined to form complete sentences.

My favourite, or rather the one I love to hate, combines a single upward nod of the head with a *tsk* sound from the mouth. It means "no," but in an of-course-not-you-idiot kind of way. When one of my teenage students used it, I thought he was actually saying "yes," because of the nod. I find it immensely irritating, and although many Neapolitans use it automatically and without meaning to be rude, I am working on eliminating it from Gino's vocabulary, at least when he's around me.

Neapolitan swearwords are colourful and profuse, causing pornographic images of body parts and religious icons to pop into my head. I take them literally, can't help myself from translating them into English. This is a big mistake since they then take on horrific proportions. They aren't meant to be analyzed and contemplated; they come and go in conversation as naturally as hello and good-bye.

Southern Italians are not soft-spoken, Gino's father being an exception. Months later when my mother comes to visit at our apartment in Meta, I hide with her in the kitchen, cowering and speculating, while Gino has what seems to be an enormous verbal altercation with the landlady. After she leaves, we rush to Gino, begging him to tell us what it was all about. Is she raising the rent? Does she disapprove of visitors? Did we commit some terrible faux pas by moving the furniture around? But no, as it turns out, she was inviting us to dinner at her house, and Gino was politely declining. She was insisting that we must come and he was insisting that we couldn't possibly fit it in, and the whole conversation sounded like Sunday morning at the soccer stadium.

The radio dial crosses a booming American voice: "Mostly sunny today with a few cloudy periods." I jump, spilling my coffee. The weather! In English! I listen intently, hanging off every delightful, intelligible word. The announcer identifies it as the station from the NATO base in Gaeta, north of Naples. Then a country song comes on. Country has always been my least favourite type of music up until this moment. The lyrics are so clear, so simple. I listen avidly to the story within the song. The words conjure up images of golden wheat fields, wild horses, and whiskey. I treasure the un-Italianness of it all!

I listen to three more songs, then, feeling as if I've found a new friend in country music, grab paper and pen and begin a list of things to do: find a job and/or advertise for private lessons, explore grocery shops, visit Gino's family, figure out what to do for the month of August. Caffeine and sugar surging through my veins, this list suddenly seems almost entirely doable today, now, in the next few hours. I will leave the visit to Gino's family until he can accompany me, but as for a job—check! I will drop off my résumé at the two local language schools. Groceries? Check! I will compare the prices and selection of the two small *fruttivendoli* in Meta with those of the large supermarket in the next town, Piano di Sorrento. Four and a half weeks away in August? Check! Gino and I will sit down over dinner to consider our options.

Our apartment is just steps from the main square, but the fact that I am forced to exit through the backdoor and walk down the steep, narrow Via Olivieri to reach it makes it seem farther. The first shop I come to is a butcher's. We eat little meat, so I pass to the first of two *fruttivendoli*.

"*Ciao, bella*," greets the shopkeeper, a man who reminds me of Adamo with his welcoming demeanour and grandfatherly warmth. "You must be a *turista*," he says, gesturing towards the crates outside his shop. "Some *melone*, perhaps, or *fichi* fresh from my brother's farm?"

I glance at the prices, which seem a little high. "I'm on my way to Piano, so perhaps I will stop on my way back. But no, I'm not a *turista*, I just moved into an apartment over there," I say, indicating our building.

"Ah, the De Falco place! And what brings you to Meta?" he asks with genuine interest, the first of many to ask me this question.

"Well, my *fidanzato* is from Naples. We both like the peninsula. I hope to find work as a teacher here."

"Ah," he sighs, a shadow passing over his wrinkled face. He grasps my left hand in his callused, stained ones and continues, "You must not live like this. You need a ring on your finger to complete your beauty. I will meet this *fidanzato* of yours and set him straight."

For a moment, I am pulled into the current of his earnestness. But then I snap back to my own reality, so different from his, and smile warmly, reclaiming my hand and promising to stop later for dinner supplies.

Next is a street leading towards the sea, and on the other side, another *fruttivendolo*, where identical fruit and vegetables are displayed, tended this time by a middle-aged woman. The prices are slightly different, some higher, some lower, and I make a mental note to stop and compare more closely on the way back.

I am becoming my mother. She always checks the flyers for each of the three local supermarkets, making a list accordingly, clipping any coupons, packing a healthy snack for the excursion, then driving from one side of town to the other and back again. The whole painful process takes all morning. I can't help but be a comparison shopper, however, especially now that Gino and I are starting a life together on a strict budget.

I take the bus to Piano, where I find that Supermercato SISA has a great selection of pasta, cheese, and wine, all of which I pile into my cart. There is even a section called *prodotti dietetici*, health food. There are bags of sugar-free puffed wheat and rice, which I suppose could constitute a good Canadian breakfast. The much larger and more appealing cookie aisle beckons, however, and I gleefully allow myself to wallow in the shameless advertising that insists *biscotti all' amarena* and chocolate shortbread are the true *prima colazione sana*, healthy breakfast. These also find their way into my cart. The fruit and vegetables are cheap but lacking in the aromatic robustness of the *fruttivendolo*'s produce. I select only a lettuce and some pears.

Laden with two large shopping bags, I get off the bus in Meta and follow the narrow street down the hill to the square. There is only one shop still open, the one I had visited earlier. The friendly *fruttivendolo* sees me coming and flashes a welcoming smile my way—a smile that is immediately extinguished when his glance falls on my bags that shout SISA in giant red letters.

I am too busy huffing and puffing my way across the cobblestones to really notice his change in attitude. Breathing a sigh, I lean my two monstrous carriers against a crate of lemons. "*Buonasera*," I say, for it is customary to greet people with "good evening" as soon as both hands of the clock pass noon. "I would like six *peperoni*, a few tomatoes, a head of garlic, and a bunch of basil."

Wordlessly, he fills my order and bids me a formal *arrivederci*. Wondering at his aloof demeanour, I go home to cook up a monstrous pot of spaghetti with peppers for dinner.

Returning from work, Gino is pleased to find the apartment full of his favourite aromas. "Ah, *casa dolce casa*," he breathes as he dumps his pack on the floor and sweeps me up in his arms. Who would have thought that my adventurous spirit would lead me across the ocean to such domesticity? Even stranger that I revel in it! Gino lifts the lid of the saucepot in order to get a better whiff. "*Sto morendo di fame*, I'm starving," he says.

The amount of food I have prepared would leave my mother speechless. There is enough spaghetti in the pot to feed my parents for a week. An overflowing bowl of olives sits on the table, and Gino has brought the usual loaf of wood-oven-baked bread from Naples. He can't bear to eat a meal without this bread. He buys it daily from his favourite *fornaio*, a hole-in-the-wall bakery down the street from the factory. The lighter bread from the peninsula just won't do, except in an emergency.

He is about to dip a huge chunk of bread into the saucepot when he stops and exclaims, "*Ma che è*? What's this? The sauce is full of yellow peppers! You've been had by the *fruttivendolo*! No one buys the yellow ones; they cause *disturbi intestinali*."

Yellow peppers? Indigestion? This is a new one on me.

"The guy was taking advantage of you because he thought you were a dumb *turista*."

"I'm afraid it might have been more than that," I say, recalling the cold shoulder I received on my return from SISA.

Gino listens to my story with a horrified expression on his face. "We will fix this," he says. "You must have a *rapporto di fiducia*, a trusting relationship, with your *fruttivendolo*; otherwise he will try to pass off all the *merda* no one else will accept. My mother has spent so many years cultivating a *rapporto di fiducia* with her *fruttivendolo* that she now has the privilege of choosing her own produce."

I think of our supermarkets back home where my mother and I, and countless other faceless shoppers, poke and prod, pick and choose to our hearts' content. Then the leftover, damaged goods are placed on a discount shelf for quick sale to those who don't mind black bruises on their bananas. If we so desire, we can complete the whole transaction, even payment, without making eye contact with another human being.

"And besides," Gino continues, "you will gain a *punto di riferimento*, someone who will always be willing to help if you need directions, information, or a consultation on how to cook zucchini flowers, for example."

I am beginning to see the error of my ways. But there is more.

"Cut the *fruttivendolo* out of your life, and you will remain forever an outsider in the community. People will already be talking about you, the new blonde *straniera* who has shacked up with a *napoletano*. This isn't Canada, it isn't even Sorrento. It's Meta, a tiny *villaggio* where everyone knows everyone else's business. You are at a severe disadvantage already; don't make it worse. Tomorrow, when I get home, we will go together and stock up on everything we can think of. We will show him that we are *persone per bene*, respectable people, and he will pass on the word. It's as simple as that."

I am silent.

"*Non preoccuparti*," he soothes, noticing my perplexed expression. "I just can't bear for you to be disrespected in any way."

I agree to the plan, while struggling with the idea of giving the *fruttivendolo* such an important role in my life. We eat the spaghetti with the delicious yellow pepper sauce but never get around to discussing plans for August. Neither one of us has *disturbi intestinali*, but I don't mention this fact.

The next day, I reluctantly tackle another item on my list—jobs. I'd rather face a thousand disgruntled *fruttivendoli* than set foot back into the clandestine work world. Fortifying myself with a second *caffè latte* and fourth chocolate cookie, I ponder the reality of my situation. I cannot allow myself to lounge around all day while Gino supports me. I feel the need to contribute financially, although Gino swears it's not necessary.

The thought of Gino's tenacity emboldens me. This time there is no official record of my entrance to Italy. I will not raise any red flags by applying for a work permit. If one of the local language schools will hire me, great. If not, I will rely on private lessons, as I know many others do. Someday, perhaps, Gino and I will marry or move to Canada, and everything will be different. For now, I must be enterprising, bold, and determined.

There is no language school in Meta, but there is one in each of the two towns between here and Sorrento. I stop first at the microscopic English Institute in Sant'Agnello. The administrator is regretful. Business has been slow, and she is finding it difficult to keep her present teachers in steady work.

Language World in Piano is bigger and more professional

looking. One floor up and overlooking the main square, it consists of a lobby, an office, and four classrooms. A friendly woman greets me and introduces herself as Signora Mosca, the school administrator. She graciously accepts my résumé and takes the time to read it through. I glance at the overflowing bookshelves that line the wall behind me. There are tapes and videos, too, things that were unheard of at the Royal School.

"We are looking for a teacher. I see you speak French—that could be a great asset as we occasionally have students who request other languages. It is also necessary to speak at least a little Italian. Our students find it helpful to be able to ask questions in their own language."

We converse for a few moments in Italian, and she seems satisfied with my capabilities. This place is worlds away from the Royal School, so businesslike and, well, normal. The pay is slightly better, too. We agree that I will observe some other teachers for two days and start with three of my own classes next week. Not exactly a full schedule, but a good start. We shake hands, and I bounce down the stairs to the square.

The sun embraces me. I want to skip, to sing out loud, but as usual, there are eyes on me so I keep my ebullience in check. A young man at the bar across the square points me out to his friends, who swivel their heads, then readjust their chairs to get a better look. Self-consciously sidling into the nearest *vicoletto*, I decide to wend my way home on foot through the tangle of streets that connect Piano with Meta.

The two towns are indistinguishable. I have no idea where one ends and the other begins. Finally, the labyrinth discharges me onto a main thoroughfare that leads to the *belvedere* overlooking the Marina di Cassano. Fishing boats rest on the sand, rainbow colours reflecting the sun. I know my way from here—ten more minutes and I will be in the Meta square. I pass restaurants, hotels, and fancy villas, all with austere iron doors or gates streetside, but with magnificent hidden terraces facing the sea. This will be my daily walk, twenty-five minutes door to door.

When Gino returns from work, I greet him with the good news.

"Don't let them *sfruttarti*," he admonishes. "Any nonsense and you're out of there, *daccordo*?"

I agree, engrossed in my gushings about the friendly administrator, the abundance of creative resources, the extra money we will have. "No more *sfruttamento* for me," I say, not sure if this word form exists, but liking the way it sounds nonetheless. The verb *fruttare* means "to fruit," so *sfruttare* is "to de-fruit." If I allow the school to *sfruttarmi*, they will be taking advantage, harvesting what fruit (or work, as the case may be) they can get for minimum remuneration. Hapless foreigners fall easily into the trap; we are simply too grateful for the opportunity to prolong our stay in paradise.

"Speaking of fruit," I say, "we need to make that trip to the shop."

Gino looks at me quizzically since he hasn't been following my linguistic train of thought. "*Si, andiamo.* We'll get some *patate* and make a *frittata*."

Potatoes are just about the last vegetable I would put in an omelette, but I have been pleasantly surprised before, with dishes like squash pasta and stuffed squid.

Gino introduces himself to the *fruttivendolo*, speaking politely and respectfully. Soon, they are chatting and laughing while I peruse the produce. I can see which are the choicest potatoes, the most luscious tomatoes; this time I will watch what we are given.

But wait! Gino is handling the vegetables himself, helping the shopkeeper pick the best of the lot. "*Quello non è buono*," he declares, nonchalantly replacing a tomato chosen by the shopkeeper. There is a momentary spark between them, and then they are smiling and slapping each other on the back.

The *fruttivendolo* bows to me. "You've got yourself a *fidanzato per bene*. All the best to both of you." And then, with great seriousness, "*Mi raccomando*, heed my words, get married as soon as possible. You'll make *bellissimi* children together!"

Chapter 20

My classes at Language World are afternoon ones, so I decide to spend my mornings swimming in Meta. Towel and air mattress in hand, I traipse down steep alleys and stairways to the Alimuri beach, nestled at the base of the giant tufo cliffs. I wear a waterproof watch Gino gave me so I can keep an eye on the time. Looking down the coast, I can see Capo di Sorrento, the ruin-studded rocky outcrop where my life here really began. It draws me even now as if to a birthplace or well-loved childhood home, full of memories and joy.

From this perspective, four miles away, the cape appears to point across the Gulf towards Naples, where Gino is ensconced in the city. He will have no view of the sea until he travels home to Meta on the train. I begin to crave his company desperately and have to force my eyes away from the city, the sea, the cape, in order to focus on the immediate, simple task of inflating my air mattress.

Potential *pappagalli* lurk near the cliffs, so I hasten to complete the job. I will feel safer in the arms of the sea. There is no one else swimming today. June is not considered summer; locals remain fully clad until August, when they ditch their clothes and jobs, heading *in massa* to the edges of Italy where they will soak up the sun on evenly spaced *lettini* for exactly one month. At the end of August, they prepare for *il rientro*, which involves piling into their cramped cars, making parking lots out of highways until they finally reach home, irascible and ready for another year of work or school.

As I wade into the gentle waves, I realize that the water is turbid. Lying flat on my air mattress, I paddle out farther, but the water remains opaque, so different from the sea on the Positano side of the peninsula. There are things floating in the water: bits of plastic, cotton swabs, a sanitary pad. This is not the first time I've seen garbage in the Mediterranean, but I am only now recognizing that perhaps I am sailing on sewage.

My stomach turns as I paddle to shore, encountering still more unsightly debris on the way. The current has carried me closer to the north end of the beach, and as I reach the shore, I notice a bedraggled mound washed up on the stones. Moving closer, I see that it is a dead dog, covered in flies.

I stop and turn away, hand over mouth and nose. At this point, the smell of rotting flesh would surely make me vomit. I picture the multitude of stray dogs in Naples, remember hearing how they are often exterminated and thrown into the sea. Did this dog meet such a fate? How many more lifeless canines are rolling silently to shore under the murky swell? I shiver, repulsed, desperately desiring a shower.

Grabbing my towel and still inflated air mattress, I climb home. I try to wash all traces of feculence from my body, all thoughts of dead dogs from my mind. Then I dry my hair, apply makeup, and dress for work. I place my waterproof watch in the top drawer of the dresser, affixing instead my usual gold and leather one. I will certainly have a use for the waterproof watch again, but never for solitary swims in Meta.

Gino is sympathetic when I tell him of my experience. "But don't worry," he says. "When we go *sott'acqua* in Positano, you will see it is a different world."

It takes a gargantuan effort just to get to the sea for our first day of snorkelling. Gino hums *"O Sole Mio"* as we assemble *panini* of *prosciutto* and artichokes. The *panini*, a jar of olives, and a bottle of red wine all go into Gino's pack. Then, in another bag, he places an inflatable dinghy, towels, a rope, and our snorkel gear.

Laden with all these necessities, we trudge up to the main road, where we wait in the square across from Santa Maria del Lauro church. Eventually, in the lumbering way of Italian buses, the big blue Sita coach wheezes up and we board, lucky enough to find seats on this, our first excursion.

From the square, the bus toils and heaves its way up the mountain to Colli di San Pietro. Here we crest the Sorrentine Peninsula, the Gulf of Salerno before us and the Bay of Naples behind. We are suspended for a moment, like an eagle poised to swoop. And then the bus dives over the crest of the mountain, hurtling towards a hairpin bend. Brakes scream as the driver spins the wheel hard to the left; the bus lurches and tilts, forcing us to the edge of nothingness. I detect the passengers who have not made this trip before; faces hidden in white hands, they dare to peek only through finger-cracks, as though this might somehow ward off a precipitous tumble to the rocks and spume below.

Just before Positano, we round a curve and come to a stop behind four cars. We can see at once what the holdup is: a motor home and a German tour bus have met on a hairpin bend. There is no room for them to pass each other, so traffic is blocked in both directions. The lanes are so narrow at this point that, although the cliff wall is on the other side of the road, I could reach out and pick wildflowers off it if I wanted to. To our right, the cliff plunges to a fjordlike cove where stray cats explore brightly painted boats on the pebble shore. A fisherman mending nets glances up at our predicament, then turns back to his work. He has seen this show before.

The drivers of the large vehicles are gesticulating and shouting. They have folded in their side view mirrors, wedged and scraped their vehicles against the rocky cliff and each other, but to no avail; there are at least six inches of unyielding metal left over. Small stones dislodged by the motor home drop over the cliff shelf, bouncing and scattering in the fjord. The cats and fisherman look up again.

More cars queue up behind us, each of them another turn in the lock that will keep us here indefinitely. The drivers behind us begin to honk. Some get out of their cars to hurl advice or obscenities. Our driver sighs, curses under his breath, and steps down from the bus.

He speaks first to the drivers of the large vehicles, then to each car driver in turn, guiding the ones behind us back to a wider stretch of road. Then he boards the bus again, maneuvering slowly backwards. I hold my breath, eyes glued to the road edge. The view below, dizzying at the best of times, is nauseating. The cars in front of us, and the motor home, crawl back, too. Our driver surveys the situation with expert eyes, making sure there is now sufficient passing room. Satisfied, he motions for the tour bus to squeeze past the motor home.

We are all frozen, willing the vehicles to somehow suck in their monstrous girths. And then the drama is over. The rescued vehicles honk a thank-you to our driver, and we are on our way again.

Once off the bus, we lug our bags down to the beach, winding our way through the precipitous maze that is Positano. From the main beach, we hike the coast trail up again, along, and finally down to Fornillo beach, our place of departure for today. Gino, still full of energy and hardly breaking a sweat, begins at once to inflate the dinghy. I sprawl on the beach, watching cars snake along the cliff road high above us. I realize then that we could have got off the bus up there and climbed down a much shorter trail.

Between breaths, Gino agrees, nonplussed. "We'll try it next time."

I can't think past today and the impending swim that will take us out past a Saracen tower to a hidden beach just west of where we are now. I glance at the other beachgoers stretched comfortably on *lettini* provided by a nearby hotel. They watch me, too, from under their *ombrelloni* and designer sunglasses. The Mediterranean is only their backdrop; many of them will never set foot in it.

Once the dinghy is inflated, Gino tosses our bags into it, ties a rope from it to himself, then assembles his gear on his body. I follow his lead, cramming my feet into the flippers, squashing the mask over my face, wedging the snorkel into my mouth. I am immobilized, a fish out of water. If I can just flop my way to the water's edge, perhaps I'll be okay. But it's worse in the shallows. Once the water covers my flippers, my feet are pinned to the bottom of the sea.

"Turn around and walk in backwards," Gino laughs.

I walk in reverse for a few steps, then slide into the sea, propelling myself out to waist depth. I practise breathing with my face in the water for a minute or two, and then we are off, skimming weightlessly out to sea. The sound of my breath in the snorkel unnerves me; it is loud and external, like the rasping of an antiquated life-support machine. But Gino is beside me, swimming slowly for my benefit. Even so, we are travelling quickly through the water. When I look up, I am amazed to see how far we have come already.

The water turns from light turquoise to darkest green. I can no longer see the bottom. A looming black shape, probably just a rock, startles me, and I rise up, gasping. I grab the dinghy and rest on its side. Gino stops and we take a break in the sun, admiring the coastline from this new perspective.

Positano is postcard perfect, a many-tiered mosaic of pastel wash and brilliant tile. Purple, pink, and orange paragliders levitate from the top of the mountain to coast on warm air before wafting and twirling towards the beach.

Partway along the headland, almost parallel with us, is a

cave. Heads above water, we swim cautiously closer and allow the waves to nudge us gently inside. We wash up on a pebbly beach, where we rest and have a look around. An ancient locked door in the wall must provide access to the Saracen tower above, now restored into a private residence. It is an enchanted, secret place, and we sit for a while in the cool dimness listening to the waves lap in and watching the distant beach activities in Positano.

Thousands of these towers ring southern Italy, some almost completely ruined, others restored and made into homes or hotels. They stand as silent sentinels now, but once, hundreds of years ago, they provided vital protection from the fearsome raids of the Saracens, invaders from the Arab world. The damp walls whisper sagas of the Middle Ages, of sacking and pillaging, brandished torches, arrows, and armour.

We feel safe here in the cave, but we would be safer up in the tower, able to scan the horizon for approaching marauders. As we wade into the sea, I wish fervently that we could explore the dark tunnelled stairway that must lie behind the door. It would surely lead us back in time and not just up to someone's fancy *salotto*.

The cave births us into the sun and open sea, where we catch our breath for a moment, blinking in the sudden brightness. Such unexpected time travel happens often in Italy: in the coliseum of Rome, in the unearthed courtyards of Pompeii. When the sea is involved, however, another dimension is added.

"It is the womb from which we were all born," Gino likes to say. "Returning to it is a wondrous *esperienza*."

I think about this as we continue on our way. I am more comfortable now with my equipment, but not entirely at ease with the seemingly endless expanse of obscurity below me. I float in Mother Earth's rolling belly, terrified to be at the mercy of the sea, but at the same time exhilarated by its immensity and quiet brooding power.

Rounding the headland, we turn towards our cove of the day. We have it completely to ourselves; it is hidden even from the road above. Fallen rocks are strewn on the beach and in the water.

During the rainy season, whole sections of the coast crumble into the sea. Today, however, all is sunny and benign as we haul the dinghy ashore. We spread our towels on the coarse sand and bask in the sun, even daring for a while, until a boat passes too close, to shed our swimsuits.

We eat part of our picnic, then doze in the shade of the cliff. Afterwards, we explore the *fondali* of the cove, following turquoise and yellow fish that dart into crevasses in the sunken boulders. Delicate sea plants float and dance with the swell. The sun coruscates through the rippling water, making a crazy checkerboard of the seafloor. I bob comfortably now in the shallows, sifting shells and stones through wrinkled mer-fingers. Gino and I play together like dolphins, diving down to the bottom, then with backs arched, arms outstretched, falling slowly up to the surface through aquamarine perfection. Rising to the beach, we let the sea-drops dry on our skin; they are salty, like tears, evaporating quickly in the sun.

We stay until the sun begins to downshift. To the west, the sea cradles tiny stars on the crest of each wave; to the east, turquoise hues deepen and mix with gold, preparing for the onset of indigo that will rise from the depths before the moon turns on its silvery light. The *Maestrale* breeze murmurs gentle blessings to the sand and rocks, leaving the world peaceful and serene in its wake.

By the time we return to Fornillo, most of the bathers have gone home. Once the sun has lost its power to tan, there are few who remain. As the bus carries us home, I point out the splendid sea colours, a rainbow made only of blues. From far out at sea, each shade becomes slightly lighter until an almost transparent hue is reached closest to shore.

Gino points to the translucent water. "Look at that heavenly colour," he says. "It's less than blue."

His English often has a way of coming out simply and perfectly poetic. I am struck by the beauty of this phrase and ponder

it as we remain propped against each other, exhausted and ful-
filled.

"Less than blue" can describe a colour, but it also speaks to
me on another level. It seems to sum up how I often feel in Italy:
sometimes not quite blue, other times worse than blue. It could
mean either, or both. Such a sublime shade could also signify
pure joy, and this, too, is what I have found in Italy.

Chapter 21

A poster hangs in a travel agent's window. Gino stops me as we walk past, drawing my attention to it. A rose-pink sand beach meets water so limpid we can see the sun's rays reflecting off the seafloor. *Sardegna, un mare di vacanze,* Sardinia, a sea of vacations, declares the poster.

"Is that beach for real?" I have never seen a pink beach before.

"That's the famous *Spiaggia Rosa.* At the northern tip of Sardegna, there is an archipelago called La Maddalena. This beach is on the tiny, uninhabited island of Budelli. There are many splendid places to visit in Sardegna. Perhaps we should go there for the month of *agosto.*"

"But how could we afford to go for a whole month?" I ache to dive into that transparent sea right now as the sun beats down, reflecting off the pavement onto my pale Canadian skin.

"*Dunque,* let's see...," muses Gino. "If we went on foot and camped, we could probably manage it. There is a ferry from Civitavecchia to Sardegna. We'd just have to get a ride to the *porto,* which is near Roma. Then, from Palau, we would take a smaller ferry to the archipelago."

Travelling on foot? Camping for a month? I would agree to just about anything to put myself in that poster.

The first day of August sees us inflating our air mattresses in the lounge aboard the Lauro Express. It is crowded and stuffy inside, but preferable to a night on deck where the strong wind prohibits sleeping *al fresco*. A combination of excitement and discomfort keeps us up most of the night. In the morning, we breakfast on *cornetti* in the ship's restaurant and watch the port of Palau come into view.

Tall silver-grey rocks, eroded into mysterious shapes, hang over the port. We disembark and await the ferry to La Maddalena. Gino carries a large backpack full of everything we, as inexperienced campers, could think of: sleeping bags, towels, swimsuits, clothes, masks and snorkels, a small burner, two small pots. Our tent and air mattresses are strapped on top. In Gino's daypack, I carry more clothes, maps, snacks, money, and a camera.

The main island of La Maddalena is clearly visible from the port of Palau. The small ferry chugs toward us and we board, along with a few other people and a couple of cars. Most of the tourists from the ship have headed to other popular Sardinian destinations, like La Costa Smeralda and the capital city of Cagliari. We stand close together against the railing, perusing the list of campgrounds Gino obtained by mail from the tourist office. We have randomly chosen one to start with and hope to use it as a base, making trips to the other tiny islands, enjoying a new beach each day.

It is a sweltering two-mile walk from the bus stop, but the campground seems acceptable. I had hoped to be closer to the sea, but it will do.

Alas, there is a hidden menace. An all-night discotheque lies just over the hill from our site. Raucous percussion blasts the tent, throbbing through the air and earth into our skulls until dawn. In the morning, bleary-eyed and cranky, we pack up and trudge back along the dusty road towards the bus stop. I am woozy from lack of sleep and the intense desertlike heat. There is no shade anywhere. No trees, just scrubby bushes emanating heady herb-scents. The heckling buzz of cicadas resonates through my exhausted brain.

Just when I think I am ready to collapse, a sign marked *spiaggia* appears. A short detour brings us to an inlet of milky blue water surrounded by a moonscape of cratered rocks. There is no one else around. We ditch our bags and clothes, immersing our tired, baked bodies. There is a claylike substance under our feet that rises in clouds when we move.

The whole trip was worth it, just for this swim. We congratulate ourselves: what luck to have found the most exquisite cove of the island on our first day! The sun seems gentler on my skin now, dancing off a layer of cool droplets. I dry off and dress, then drape my towel over a prickly bush. The scent of sunbaked herbs rises to my nostrils. My stomach starts to rumble. Gino hears.

"There was an *alimentari* near the bus stop. We can get some *panini* while we wait."

I am reluctant to leave this otherworldly utopia, but I am ravenous. The herb scent is intoxicating; I desire huge slabs of *formaggio*, chased by great cool glasses of *vino*. I re-slather myself with sunscreen and pull my white cotton sun hat over my dripping hair. The hat had been just a little too tight, so I cut it up the back, sewing in a section of white glove-lining fabric.

"If Roberto ever sees that hat, he'll have a stroke!" Gino laughs.

Roberto would be scandalized, not only by the unorthodox, unattractive use of glove lining, but by the way it shouts "German tourist." Even more than Americans, Germans are known in Italy for their lack of fashion sense. It is not a compliment that I am often mistaken for a German.

"Don't worry, my little *tedesca*," says Gino. "I will protect you from ridicule." There is pride in his voice, and I know, hat or no hat, there is no one he would rather have with him, right here, right now.

We resume our walk to the bus stop. A constant breeze, seeming to radiate from some inland furnace, dries my soaked hat and hair almost instantly. Such moistureless, searing heat is new to me. It even emanates in waves from the parched earth. There is no escape from it.

"The secret is to stay in the water as much as possible," says Gino, who has hardly broken a sweat under the monstrous backpack. "We must find a campground closer to the beach." He wears no hat or sunglasses. Sometimes he allows me to apply the odd dab of sunscreen, but insists it's not necessary. Like all Mediterranean people, Gino was born with a tan that varies from espresso in the summer to *caffè latte* in the winter, but which never fades entirely.

The shutters of the *alimentari* are drawn against the sun, but it is open. Stepping into the welcome shade, we are greeted by sumptuous odours of ripe cheeses and smoked meats. Standing as close as possible to the cool glass of the deli counter, I wait in weak-kneed anticipation as Gino orders a large chunk of Sardinian sheep's cheese. He buys a loaf of grainy bread to go with it and an ice-cold bottle of water.

There is no bus shelter, so we sit on a bench under the shop's awning. I hold the bottle of water against my face while Gino prepares sandwiches. As we eat, we discuss our next move. We are not sure which campground to try and are randomly selecting from the list when a young man appears from around the corner. Seeing our list, he advises us wholeheartedly to try Camping Abbatoggia.

"It's near the sea, nice beaches, a fabulous spot."

We want more details, but the bus arrives.

"Camping Abbatoggia?" Gino asks.

The driver nods, and we board.

The bus deposits us in a swirling cloud of grit at the northwestern tip of La Maddalena. I am sorry to be so far from our idyllic cove and apprehensive about the conditions we might find in this new *campeggio*. But it is an easy downhill walk from the bus stop, and I can see that this place is indeed very close to the water.

In fact, the campground straddles a small peninsula, with dazzling seascapes all around. The breeze is stronger here, but cooler, breathed from Le Bocche di Bonifacio, the tempestuous strait between Sardinia and Corsica. Amazingly, there is shade. Not provided by trees, but by wide tarps patchworked together and strung up on poles to make a green roof over the entire campground.

We sign in at the office, then work our way through the tight grid of tents until we reach a free space. I can't believe that we will be able to touch our neighbours on both sides, but I have given up dreaming of Canadian campgrounds, where raccoons are the only nocturnal disturbance.

After setting up our tent, we explore the environs of Camping Abbatoggia. There are bathrooms with plenty of showers, a small grocery shop, a games room, and most importantly, splendid beaches flanking both sides of the peninsula. In one cove lies a small rocky island, swimming distance away, begging to be explored. Another beach is made up entirely of tiny coloured shells, jewels to sift through fingers on a lazy afternoon. At the tip of the peninsula is more lunar-grey rock, which will shift to Martian red at sunset. Already the morning's cove has paled in memory. These are truly poster-perfect beaches; we could spend the whole month here and never have to move.

The wind blows steadily throughout our first night at Abbatoggia, but we sleep well, our flimsy tent somewhat protected by those around us. In the morning, we make tea on our small burner, spread jam on unleavened Sardinian bread, and carry our breakfast to the hill overlooking the closest beach. Alive with sunrise and expectation, we plan a swim out to the island and a trip into town for supplies. The weeks ahead glisten enticingly with aquamarine adventures.

We are soon on a first-name basis with the bus driver who takes us on daily excursions around La Maddalena or over the causeway to Caprera, an island reserve of pure nature, soaring cliffs, pine forests, and hidden coves. Each beach we find is better than the last, a remarkable ascent to perfection that reduces our first milky inlet to a muddy sinkhole.

The town of La Maddalena has an isolated, holiday feel to it. We discover a bakery that sells delicious *formagelle* tarts made with ricotta and raisins, and *focaccia* sprinkled with rosemary. This latter we take with us to Enoteca Lio, where we buy glasses of *vermentino*, a local white wine, on tap. A sign encourages patrons to bring their own snacks, fill their own bottles. We find a table in the cavernlike room where we sip our cool wine, tear into the crusty *focaccia*, and revel in dankness only the sun-scorched can truly appreciate. The *vermentino* is so refreshing we make a mental note to return armed with empty water bottles.

We book a boat tour on one of the many vessels vying for business in the port. Aboard *Il Delfino Bianco* we sail to the semi-deserted island of Santa Maria, where we picnic and wander the beach like castaways. Later, we leap gleefully from the boat into blue-green depths near the protected island of Budelli. The sand glows pink in the sun, but we are not allowed to approach; the beach is eroding, partly due to the pocketfuls of sand tourists were carrying away. I understand the urge to capture perfection. My body wants to absorb these colours, take them home, and add them to the forest-greens, browns, and ochres of my homeland.

Many days, we stay close to Abbatoggia, exploring the peninsula, making it our own. We collect sea sponges and shells, discover ruins and caves, then for dinner each evening we pack a picnic and hike to the tip of the peninsula. Seated solidly on the Earth as it rolls away from the sun, we absorb the last red rays and descend, with Sardinia, into night.

Chapter 22

We arrive home from Sardinia tanned and tired. I head straight for the bathroom to take a shower and admire my tan lines. But where the hall to the bathroom used to be, there is now a wall. I can just see the outline of the arch, but it has been bricked up, plastered, and whitewashed to near-invisibility.

"Gino!" I shout. "Our bathroom's gone!"

From somewhere far away, Gino calls back, "There's another one down here!"

In my hurry to get to the shower, I hadn't noticed that the mysterious downstairs room had been opened up. The huge slab of wood at the bottom of the stairs is gone, so I follow Gino's voice down and into the enormous room. I touch the smooth oak dining table; it is even larger than it appeared through the crack. Two single beds are tucked into a far corner beside the bathroom. A double glass door leads into a courtyard.

Gino is as surprised as I am. We look at each other in confusion. Our bathroom is now three rooms and a stairway farther away from where it was, but we have all this newfound space.

"Look at that," Gino says, pointing to the wall behind me.

"A fireplace!" I coo, turning to run my hand along the wooden mantle. "I wonder if we're allowed to use it!"

Just then, Signor De Falco knocks at our new door. He steps in hesitantly, formally, as though he hasn't been here every day for the past month reorganizing our home. Full of apologies, Signor De Falco explains that he is renovating the apartment next to ours. Since it didn't have a *bagno* and since ours had *due,* he made some modest adjustments. I forgive him for the distant bathroom when he tells us the fireplace works and we are welcome to use it.

"But firewood is scarce around here," he says apologetically.

I see a twinkle in Gino's eyes, and after Signor De Falco leaves, he tells me his plan: "I'll get a saw. We can collect fallen logs from *la pineta.*"

His enthusiasm is not dampened by my remark that we don't yet have a car, *la pineta* is at the top of the mountain range while our apartment is at the bottom, and rotting pine wood doesn't burn worth *merda.*

After twice hacking and packing fungus-encrusted logs into our canvas bag and hauling them home on the bus, only to have them sizzle and smoke, Gino gives up, turning instead to the tried-and-true method of collecting driftwood from the beach. This, too, is a struggle, however, since tides are almost nonexistent and great driftwood-tossing storms are infrequent. There is no other heat source in the house besides the pizza oven that also requires wood, so Gino begins squirrelling away everything burnable we find on our hikes. We now come home laden, not only with herbs, but with olive branches, pinecones, and cardboard.

Signor De Falco doesn't claim our rent as income, so we cannot receive mail at the apartment. Nor can we have the phone in our name or our own label beside one of the three doorbells outside. The apartment is in his son's name; everything must appear as though we are not actually occupying the space. So we have our mail sent to Gino's parents in Naples and inform everyone we know which doorbell to press. As for the phone, since we don't have connections at SIP, the Italian phone company, it takes a whole month to get one installed. During this month we are forced to use the disgustingly damp and sticky pay phone in the square.

Hiding rental income is just one of many ways people in southern Italy defraud the government. The state has always been corrupt, so why shouldn't the citizens look out for themselves? No one thinks it's wrong to cheat on taxes. The government expects evasion and makes taxes even higher to compensate for all the cheating. It's a vicious cycle.

"It would be different if we actually saw results," says Gino. "But we pay and pay and get *niente* in return. In fact, it's worse than getting *niente*. It's like paying someone to do you harm."

He's referring in part to the pitiful state of health care in the south, to the almost complete lack of social services, and to the red tape that will ensnare you until you writhe and scream in frustration. Just try to start a business, buy property, or register a car through the proper legal channels. It's virtually impossible, so no one tries.

When I tell Gino how uncorrupt Canadians are compared to Italians, he explains that Italians can't rely on their government to look out for them, so they look out for themselves. "In Canada, you receive something for your money. Your taxes pay for quality health *servizi*, education, and maintenance of towns and cities. You don't have to bribe someone every time you need a job done."

I can see how strongly he feels, as he takes a breath and continues passionately, "When you were thrown out of Italia, that wasn't the law at work. That was just one department pretending to function by taking on the easiest job available. *Nessuno* cared if you were here, they just found your case less *arduo* than dealing with drug lords and Mafia hit men."

I understand now that Italians need to be very clever or very powerful in order to have such lawlessness work for them rather than against them.

"For most of us," says Gino, "it is a daily struggle just to keep our heads above water."

For me, it's more like a constant attempt to remain blended with the masses, while never taking even a small step into the system, never putting my name on a form, never filing a complaint. I manage to fly below the radar at work. I do my job and keep quiet about my status. The rest of the teachers belong to the European Economic Community, so there is little to bring the authorities sniffing around. For now, I am safe within the chaos.

Two contracts come up at work, and I am assigned to both of them. One because it involves teaching French at an elementary school, something only I am qualified to do, and the other simply because no one else wants it. For the French job, I will just have to travel a few stops by bus or train to Sorrento. For the other, teaching advanced English, I will be taking the train to an electrical factory in Leopardi, a squalid drug-ridden town halfway around the bay towards Naples, and directly under Vesuvius.

My first day on the English job, I step onto the outdoor platform of Leopardi station. I'm not in the shadow of Vesuvius simply because the sun is shining towards me across the sea, but the volcano is right there, towering above me.

"Wait at the station," Signora Mosca had warned. "There will be someone from the factory to meet you. Leopardi is not a place to wander around alone."

Sure enough, a neatly dressed young man is waiting.

"My name is Antonio. Please allow me to accompany you to your assignment."

I am, perhaps foolhardily, relieved by his appearance and formal greeting. We shake hands, and he leads me, not to a car, but to a monstrous motorcycle.

Coming from a country where winter lasts for six months of

the year, I have had little exposure to motorcycles. Hiking my medium-length skirt into a micro-mini, I climb on and clamp my arms around Antonio, embarrassed by this sudden close contact with a stranger.

The traffic is bumper-to-bumper, but he weaves his way through as though cars, buses, and motor scooters are only harmless pylons. When there is a free spot, we travel on the wrong side of the road. Coming face-to-face with a bus, I grip him even tighter, glancing around to see another bus coming up beside us. I bury my face in Antonio's back; he shifts gears and glides expertly between the two. By the time we reach the factory, my insides are a blubbering mess. I leap to the ground, throwing the motorcycle and Antonio off balance, knocking both to the ground.

"You're not used to riding on motorcycles, are you?" he asks breathlessly, struggling to right the colossal machine.

"Not really," I mumble, smoothing my skirt.

Antonio leads me into the administrative wing of the factory. My classroom is a large, bright conference room with a long meeting table, comfortable chairs, and an enormous whiteboard. There is one other student waiting.

"*Ciao, Giovanni*," says Antonio. "I present to you our new English teacher, Signorina Wright."

Giovanni stands to shake my hand. He is also neatly dressed and clean shaven, not what I had expected from factory workers in Leopardi.

It turns out there are just the two of them for my course of advanced English. Signora Mosca will be disappointed with the attendance, but as long as the company pays the full fee, she will keep sending me. In spite of the horrific motorcycle ride, I look forward to the next class. These students are a pleasure to teach, even more polite than the waiters I taught at the Royal School. And I will be reimbursed for travel time, a huge bonus.

There are no incidents on the way back to the train station, but Antonio and I are both relieved when it rains the next week and he has an excuse to bring his car.

The French job is more labour intensive. I have never taught Italian children; they are neither polite nor respectful. I have to come up with rhymes and songs and games in order to keep their attention. There aren't many resources available, so I spend hours outside work making my own materials. Signora Mosca eventually agrees to pay me for extra planning time, but it is never enough. I enjoy getting out, however, and being paid for expenses and meals.

Travelling around, for work and for pleasure, comes a little easier once we acquire Ettore's old *Seat*. I am even able to drive myself to Leopardi, directly along the *autostrada*, and leave the car in the factory's safely guarded employee parking lot. But while I no longer have to rely on buses and trains, I find my nerves will take some toughening before driving in Italy becomes anything less than terrifying.

I remember straight Canadian roads with hardly a car in sight. I remember traffic lights and stop signs, lines painted on the road to indicate passing lanes, horns used only when absolutely necessary.

Italy is chaotic by comparison. There are traffic lights in Naples, but they are more for decoration than anything else. Drivers watch other cars, not the lights. If there is a space large enough to pass through, they surge onward, palm on the horn, feet working nimbly on accelerator, brake, and clutch. It is a wild dance, choreographed to earsplitting music.

On the peninsula, there is one lone traffic light, on a relatively quiet street in Meta, near the sea. It takes me some time to be able to ignore it. But then I realize it is safer not to stop; driving cautiously will only have me rear-ended. This is often the fate of unsuspecting foreigners who obey the lights in Naples. Drivers in Meta and Sorrento are less aggressive, but still firm believers in the power of the honk. When approaching a blind intersection, right-of-way is signalled by a couple of quick blats on the horn. If some rare error occurs, drivers just slam on the brakes and swear profusely. I will never get the hang of this madness; I am unable to trust this nonsystem that seems to work for everyone else.

It's not just other cars I have to deal with; motor scooters, pedestrians, and stray dogs all add to my stress level. There are no apparent rules for motor scooters. They weave in and out, go against the flow, ride up on the sidewalk. I learn to expect old ladies with bundles of groceries or groups of gossiping teens to step out unannounced at any moment. The same goes for stray dogs. There is no time for daydreaming or gazing at the view. I become a better driver, more attentive, with quicker reflexes, but not having been born into this chaos, I find coping comes hard and driving is rarely a pleasure for me.

What I do enjoy is the freedom. There is a parking lot at SISA, one of the few in the area. I can load up on groceries without having to wrestle with bags on the bus. Or, if I am really ambitious, I can drive up the highway to the *supermercato* at Pompeii, where, under one roof, lies an enormous selection of everything from fish to electric blankets and fax machines. Best of all, we are free from bus schedules on the weekends. We can drive to Positano, or farther south to places like Paestum and Palinuro, stopping along the way when we feel like it to pick chestnuts, buy fresh buffalo mozzarella, or just admire the view. Closer to home, we can go for a spontaneous hike in the *pineta* or for a late-night pizza at *da Salvatore* without relying on friends for transportation.

Gino still takes the train to work. It works out to be cheaper, it's often more relaxing, and there is less chance our car will be stolen or vandalized. The Fiat *Uno* is the model of choice for car thieves, but there is no guarantee that Gino, exiting from the factory in the evening, will find the *Seat* where he left it. Fortunately for us, our car is entirely unremarkable, almost invisible—suitably bashed up, dirty, with a removable radio that we always take with us, no luxuries. It is a far cry from the sparkling new-edition *Seat* we once rented for a drive to Assisi. Fun to drive, yes, but a constant worry every time we left it.

In Naples, men will approach out of nowhere and offer to watch your parked car for a fee. Pay five thousand lire to one of these illegal attendants, and you will most likely find your car where you left it, wheels and windows intact, with no more scratches than one would expect from an outing in Naples.

If you refuse to pay, the *guardiano* will turn a blind eye while thieves and vandals help themselves to your vehicle. He may even call up his cousin, a dealer in black-market hubcaps or transmissions. These crimes occur in broad daylight, on streets and in spaces where one would normally expect to park legally. Some of these *guardiani* have regular clients who even trust them to find a parking space, tossing over the keys as they hurry off to an appointment.

I steer clear of the whole scene. I let Gino drive in Naples, or we take the train and walk.

When a short contract comes up to teach English at an elementary school in Priora, a tiny village up the mountain from Capo di Sorrento, I accept, as usual.

The road is full of hairpin bends, but traffic is light and I am able to admire the view. Brilliant green and silver olive trees stand in a thick carpet of golden broom, which cascades terrace by terrace towards the sea, towards Capo, where Gino and I first met. I have to pull myself back from blissful reverie, from the fierce urge to just keep driving and exploring rather than working.

I park beside a gigantic dumpster outside the school. It is lunch hour; shrieking children run wildly around a fenced courtyard bordered by a dazzling grove of lemons. Each perfect fruit seems to be imbued with a light of its own, like so many tiny suns nestled in an emerald universe.

A bell summons the children inside. Some linger, watching me approach. I fumble with the gate, which is locked. The children stare, wide-eyed. They pretend not to understand when I call for help, giggling at my accent. Finally, one of them shouts for a teacher, who comes to let me in.

I introduce myself, expecting the usual courtesy. There is none. Only a grudging *venite*, follow me, no eye contact. The teacher leads me to a classroom where all hell is breaking loose.

Dishevelled, half-dressed children are everywhere—on the desks, under the desks, on the windowsill. They bicker, tumble, wrestle, throw. Unbelievably, a teacher sits on the other side of the room, marking papers. I am alone now in the doorway, so I move towards him, fighting my way through desks crammed so tightly I have to crush myself up against the blackboard to reach him. He looks up questioningly, unsmiling, as if he has no idea why I am here. I explain over the ruckus.

He shrugs, then stands up. "*State zitti, imbecili!* Shut up, idiots!"

I flinch. His booming voice is so full of hatred it makes me cringe. The children ignore him.

"I said shut up you stupid cretins! Now sit down before I smack you all into tomorrow!"

The children reluctantly begin to assemble at their desks. The room remains a war zone of crumpled papers and half-empty backpacks. The teacher squeezes past me, exiting silently.

Through my fog of shock, I realize I have about 0.3 seconds to grab their attention. I kick myself into educator/entertainer mode, dividing up the room into two teams. The idea of a competition interests them. They are unused to learning through games, and I can sense that they feel they are getting away with something, that I am a complete dupe. I am constantly on the verge of losing control of them, but we make it through, with only a couple of fistfights breaking out.

For the last ten minutes, I have them sit down and complete a simple exercise sheet. I tell them it is still part of the game, that I will only be able to tally the teams' scores once it is complete. With the exception of a few dissidents, the class complies, noisily working together in fierce rivalry. I relax just a little, knowing I will soon be free. Outside the window, the lemon paradise beckons to me. I want to jump out, never to return.

The teacher comes back, and I shout over the din for a boy to collect the sheets and bring them to me. The boy trips over a chair, spilling the papers onto the floor. A roar of laughter rises wildly, hysterically. The teacher reaches across the desks, grabs the boy by the collar, and hauls him to the front.

While the teacher shouts obscenities, I see his hand rise, and I can't believe he's going to strike the child, but he does, violently, across the face, leaving a white slash that quickly turns scarlet. I feel sick. I want to help, or run.

I am disgusted by the behaviour of this man, but there is one thing that completes the horror of the scene: the nonreaction of the boy. My heart freezes in the realization that this treatment is normal for him. He stands limply, eyes blank, collar stretched tight, still in the hand of the man.

Then the bell rings. My game and the scores are forgotten. The scrape and squeal of chairs fills the room as the students make their escape, at least for a while. The man shoves the boy roughly towards the door, then leaves without another word.

I need to react, to tell someone, to fix the situation. As I leave, I see the man in the principal's office, laughing with other staff. I turn away, boiling with emotions I've never felt before.

I climb mechanically into my car and return to Language World. Signora Mosca is there. I walk into her office, close the door, and spill the whole story.

She listens carefully, but the look on her face makes me feel like one who has led a far-too-sheltered existence. "I'm sorry for your discomfort, Sheila, but there are traditions, especially in the hill towns, that we cannot change."

I want to be indignant, righteous, stronger than tradition. But I'm not. I'm exhausted, impotent.

"If you wish to forfeit the contract, I can assign it to someone else, someone with fewer cultural differences."

I want nothing more than to erase the memory of this day, so I accept her offer and hand over my lesson plans.

I pick over the memory, however, bit by bit, and by the time Gino gets home, I am wadded up in an angry knot. The story comes out again, more detailed and horrific than the first time. "Child abuse is a crime! Can we go to the police?"

Before he answers, I already know that, firstly, we must both stay away from the police, and secondly, they wouldn't do anything anyway, having most likely been raised with the same type of discipline.

My disenchantment with Italy hangs over our heads for the next week. And to make matters worse, I have a new stalker. Not a gentle, charming one like Costantino, but a creepy, make-your-skin-crawl, motorcycle-riding *rattuso*. He hangs out at the corner with his friends, dark glasses balanced absurdly on his forehead. He stares pointedly at me, makes what he thinks are seductive noises, then follows. I could take the car to work, but I prefer to walk. The route is scenic and good exercise. Also, by the time I manoeuvre the car out of its tight spot, fight traffic, then find another parking spot near the school, I could have walked twice.

Most of the *pappagalli* know me, have given up on me, like the one who followed my bus to Colli and a small sweaty man who used to pant after me, "You go to beach? You go to beach?" But this one is different. He has seen me with Gino, has heard me decline his sleazy invitations a hundred times, yet he won't give up. He's obviously bored, probably unemployed. Chasing me is a delicious distraction.

Passing the corner has become a torture. I don't want to make a big deal of it to Gino; I'm afraid of how he might react. In an effort to reason with the creep, I stop, make eye contact, and beg him to leave me alone. I lie and tell him that I am married, that my husband will be furious, but there is nothing in his eyes except darkness. I walk away. He follows.

So, through tears of frustration, I tell Gino. And I tell him more: how I miss being unremarkable, how I want to be paid what I'm worth, how I miss my family and friends, how I want a couch and a bathtub, for God's sake! I weep and grieve for all the things I miss, complain of all the negatives, unable to see at this moment, all of Italy's glorious positives. "I want to go home. To Canada. With you," I moan.

Gino calms me. He wants me to be happy. "Tell me more about your *paese*. My short visit at Easter gave me only the smallest taste of what living there might be like."

I tell him. And he listens, but I know he doesn't get it, just as I didn't get southern Italy before I lived here. It was pasta and wine and sunshine and people with big hearts and huge families. I found all that, but I found so much more and so much less.

Canada can be less, too, but I am now caught within the nostalgic perception that comes with being away. I make the blackflies and mosquitoes disappear; I forget to mention the January winds that saw into exposed flesh like a serrated knife while you chisel two inches of ice off your car. Instead, I paint a picture of autumn leaves, gentle breezes, solitude, and tranquillity. Gino's imagination takes it all in, mixing it with years of exposure to American films and spaghetti westerns.

"We'll talk more about moving, if that's what you really want. But first," he states coolly, "I will speak with this *rattuso*."

I'm tired. I don't care. It is night now, and I just want to go to sleep.

The next day, Gino and I drive past the square. It's a sunny Saturday morning, and we are on our way to Positano. I feel better than I did last night, but there is a cloud in my head that won't let me focus clearly on what I really want. The creep is there, pretending not to see us.

Gino pulls over right beside him and gets out of the car. The ice in his eyes belies his courteous tone: "I believe you've met my wife."

"*Si*, I think I've seen her around."

"I'm sure you wouldn't be harassing her, *vero?*" Gino moves his tall presence just a little closer to the other man.

"Why of course not," the creep lies. "I don't know what you're talking about."

"*Bene*," says Gino. "I'm glad there will be no trouble."

They look at each other for a moment, and the pact is sealed. Neither of them has spoken the truth, yet they have understood each other perfectly.

The next Monday as I pass the man, I avert my gaze as usual, but watch out of the corner of my eye. I hear nothing, see nothing but the almost imperceptible, respectful nod of his head. I continue on my way, steps lighter, Italy brighter.

Chapter 23

"*Ecco il gattino*," says Ciro's mother, Francesca, as she hands me a bony kitten covered from head to paw in a horrible scabby crust. Even his miniscule nose appears deformed.

"He has a little skin condition," she continues. "But he's really very sweet. Watch how he plays with this rolled-up plastic bag."

I place the tiny creature on the floor of Francesca's kitchen. It fixes watering eyes beseechingly upon me and pointedly ignores the bag.

I hear Gino's voice in my head: "No cats." I had complained of needing company on the lonely evenings when he works late or goes to karate. Never having grown up with a pet, he has no idea that acquiring one can be a simple yet fulfilling venture. I tried to explain this, but he remained adamant, bogged down in details. "No, *amore mio*. What happens if we move to Canada? We certainly couldn't take a cat with us. You'd be attached to it, and there'd be heartache. No, we just can't get involved with *animali*."

I heard his words, but remixed them in my mind to mean, "Find a cat, bring it home, and everything else will sort itself out."

When Arianna called and told me Francesca had found a kitten trapped inside her garden wall, I rushed right over. And now I stand in her doorway, ready to leave with a stripey grey mite under one arm and a bag of cat food under the other.

"Remember to moisten the food," says Francesca. Then she hands me the wadded-up plastic bag. "Here, take his favourite toy as well."

When Gino comes home, I pull him into the study. "I have a surprise for you," I say, leading him to the basket where our kitten lies curled, blue saucer-eyes imploring for approval.

Gino looks at me, but I avoid his gaze, busying myself with the dishes of cat food on the floor. He reaches out to the kitten and picks it up. "*Dio mio!*" he exclaims. "This cat needs to be treated at once for fungus!"

I take his reaction as a sign that he is about to be won over, so I turn my own sweetest expression on him. "You can name him if you like."

He looks doubtful and then, as the kitten begins to purr, burrowing itself into the crook of his arm, resigned. He replaces the cat in the basket and regains his man-of-the-house stance. "We'll call him *Tigrotto*, little tiger. But don't get too attached. He's not coming to Canada. You'll have to find a home for him. I'll pick up some anti-fungal shampoo tomorrow, and you can get started on cleaning the poor *bestia*."

As Gino goes off to wash his hands, I imagine a wink from Tigrotto. We both know that if there is a move to Canada, Tigrotto will indeed be coming along.

I had thought Tigrotto was mostly scab and bones, but now that I have him pinned in the outdoor sink, it turns out he's made entirely of claws and teeth. Within a matter of seconds, he has punctured so many holes in my rubber gloves, the suds from the toxic antifungal shampoo begin to slosh freely around my fingers. I finally manage to lather him up, but the instructions say that the suds must sit for five minutes before rinsing. What to do with a frantic wet kitten for five minutes?

I will have to hold him for the duration, so I put him on a towel on my knee, trying not to rub any of the shampoo off. He squirms constantly, desperate to get away. At one point, he makes a dash for the undergrowth, and I grab him by his slippery tail. After an interminable five minutes, I rinse every drop of shampoo off his skin, something that proves more difficult than the lathering. He is convinced I'm trying to drown him and puts up a fight worthy of ten tigers. Finally, the job is finished, and he stalks into the sun to shake and lick.

I put the cap on the bottle and glance again at the instructions: "Repeat twice a day for two weeks."

Over the next months, Tigrotto grows from a scrawny mite to a lanky, muscular feline. His favourite indoor activities include ankle-biting and watching the laundry slosh and flop in the front-loading machine. Outdoors, he ventures farther and farther away. Sometimes, I catch sight of him springing onto the neighbour's balcony and up to the roof before disappearing from view. I worry about stray dogs and fast cars, but when I call his name, he always materializes from over the garden wall or out from under Signor De Falco's tomato plants.

One day, however, I call and call, but Tigrotto doesn't come. When Gino gets home, he goes into the garden, whistling the two notes, one high, one low, that Tigrotto always responds to. Still no sign. For three days I wait and worry, sure he has been attacked by a dog or run over by a car.

Then on the fourth afternoon, I see his shape outside the glass door. I throw it open, ready for him to bound inside, but he staggers instead, barely able to cross the threshold before collapsing on the tiles. I pick him up gently and examine him for injuries. The first thing I notice is that his skin and eyes are yellow; this sickly colour combined with his weakness terrifies me.

I take him right away to the vet, a friendly, caring woman who neutered him a few months earlier. Tigrotto normally hates riding in the car, protesting physically and vocally, but now he lies motionless on the passenger seat. It breaks my heart to see him like this.

The vet can tell right away that he has a feline flu. "We must hook him up immediately to an intravenous drip." She calls the intravenous drip, *lavaggio di sangue*, which translates literally as "blood wash."

I feel so helpless, I will agree to anything. She injects him with a tranquillizer, then inserts a tiny needle into his paw. She tapes the needle in place, then attaches it to a thin plastic tube. The tube is connected to a bag of clear fluid, which the vet tells me must be kept elevated. I wonder why she is telling me this, for obviously she is the one looking after him.

After ten minutes, she unplugs the tube, leaves the needle in his paw, and places tiny plastic caps on both the tube and the needle. She lifts Tigrotto into my arms, places the bag of fluid on top of my limp cat, and leads me to the door.

"Plug it in again when you get home, then take it out for the night so he can get up and walk around if he is able. Bring him back in the morning, and we'll see how he's doing."

I am speechless with trepidation. An intravenous drip should only be administered by trained medical professionals! In my panic I fail to perceive that, in a country where distrust of the medical system causes people to take health care into their own hands, washing the blood of cats must be considered a mere triviality.

Gino is home from work, so I only have to buzz and the door opens for us. I had forgotten to call him or leave a note; the worry on his face turns to surprise and shock as he helps us inside.

When I tell him the story and the vet's instructions, he swings into action, preparing a makeshift intravenous stand out of an upside-down broom tied to a chair. He folds a thick towel and places it on the gigantic glass and oak table in our living room.

My stomach is in knots as I take the caps off and try to connect the tube with the needle in Tigrotto's paw. I feel the delicate vein below his yellow skin, and I just can't bring myself to apply pressure.

Gino takes the tube from me and with a firm, steady motion, it's done. Tigrotto hasn't even moved.

Gino and I sit together silently, almost hypnotized by the rhythmic drip of the fluid. I remember the day my pony, my best friend through my childhood years, slit his throat on a metal gate. I thought I would lose him until the vet discovered that his jugular vein was intact and he would survive with stitches and stall rest. All I could do was stroke my pony in an effort to comfort him while he dripped blood on my shoes and the vet tended his gaping wound.

I have been stroking Tigrotto's head, but now I still my hands and lay them on his torso, not really for comfort, since he is sedated and relaxed, but because I feel a pull; my hands *want* to be there. Immediately I sense a transmission of energy, a communication of my own vitality to his body. And whether I'm healing him or the *lavaggio* is taking effect, five minutes later Tigrotto stirs, opens his eyes, and sits up. He looks around almost brightly, but remains calmly seated on his towel. I take my hands off his body, knowing that he is going to be okay.

In the morning, Gino drives to the vet while I hold Tigrotto in a cardboard box on my knee. Our cat is so close to being back to normal that he claws a hole in the box, bites me on the hand, then flies around the car like a mad thing before entangling himself in Gino's lower legs.

"*Che cazzo!*" Gino curses loudly as the car swerves, scraping against a stone wall. He continues to curse the rest of the way to the vet's, while I try to restrain a yowling wildcat under the quickly shredding cardboard, wishing fervently that I had worn gloves.

"This is miraculous!" exclaims the vet. "You must have a special gift with animals," she says, looking at me.

I had thought so myself, but now, as she examines Tigrotto, he squirms violently under my hands, the sharp parts of his body making painful contact with the tender ones on mine. His gratitude is not evident.

"Take him home. He will be fine." She waves to us as we drive away, Tigrotto wailing his indignation as I stuff him into the remains of the box.

Chapter 24

My father is our first international visitor. I know that, for him, Venice has always been on a short list of see-before-you-die places. He is a man of few wants. In fact, we had always been hard-pressed to buy gifts for him; he was not rich and certainly not materialistic; he was simply content. Now I have a chance to grant him a wish.

When we invite him to stay with us in Meta and travel to Venice with me, I half expect him to decline, to say he is too old and tired, but he accepts wholeheartedly. My parents agree that this will be my father's special time and that my mother will take her turn later. For now, she will stay at home to care for the house, dog, and cat.

Once the flight is confirmed, I panic. I have rarely seen my father outside his own environment, where his ways are set in stone, no questions asked. We travelled together only once, when I was fifteen, on a two-week trip to the Atlantic coast of Canada. My father was in full control the whole time, following precisely the detailed maps laid out for him by the Canadian Automobile Association. I napped in the backseat of the car, confident that he would not only bring us safely to our destination, but that he would provide me with food, a place to sleep, and anything else

I might desire. Now, my knowledge of Italian and my experience in Italy put me in the driver's seat.

For as long as I can remember, my father has had a nightly soak in the bathtub before preparing a bedtime snack of toast and peanut butter. Then he lounges on the couch, eating his toast and reading the paper.

"We don't have a bathtub, a toaster, or a couch!" I moan. "There isn't even a jar of peanut butter within two hundred miles!"

"I'm sure the good things will outweigh the bad," says Gino. "Being with you, his only daughter, a trip to Venice, and all the Chianti he can drink—what could be better?"

I ask around anyway, for the loan of a toaster. There are none to be found. Gino constructs a couch out of two bed frames roped together, covered with mattresses and a large swathe of red fabric from the factory. It actually looks passable, and we place it in front of the fireplace so my father can enjoy the warmth and atmosphere after his shower. I fan the flames of my anguish by dwelling on the thought of sharing a bed with Gino while my father sleeps in the next room. How will I look him in the eye as we say good-night? How awkward will our toastless breakfasts be?

It is a warm November day when my father arrives in Rome. Gino and I have been together for exactly a year, and I am exuberant. The *Seat* is undergoing repairs; Gino's friend, Angelo, drives us to the airport in his car so my father won't have to wait for a connecting flight to Naples. When my father appears in the crowd of arriving travellers he seems so out of context, so helpless, completely in my hands. I am alarmed. How will I manage alone with him in Venice?

The sun beats down on the airport parking lot. My father has always been a shade-seeker. I want to rush him to our cool apartment, but then perhaps it will be too cold and damp for him there. We can light a fire, but what if the wind changes and fills the place with smoke?

Angelo drives ninety-five miles per hour all the way to Naples. Gino tries to make small talk, and my father comments politely, keeping one eye on the highway, white knuckles gripping the armrest. I sit tensely in the back seat. I hate going this fast, and I'm sure my father is hating it too.

As we round the bay towards Sorrento, Angelo is forced by traffic to slow down. Gino points out Vesuvius, Pompeii, and Capri. The scent of pine groves and orange blossoms fills the car. I begin to relax.

At home, we order pizza from a restaurant up the street and eat it with a bottle of Chianti, on the cool marble table, soft light from the antique candelabra casting our shadows up to the vaulted ceiling. My father can relax now, too. He swears he will never again be able to eat Canadian pizza, with its thick, tasteless crust and rubbery cheese.

Tigrotto takes to my father immediately. Twice as big as he was when we adopted him, he is still scrawny and full of kittenish antics. My father films him climbing the palm tree in the courtyard, leaping onto unsuspecting lizards, bringing the tails home as trophies. At night, by the fire, Tigrotto curls up on my father's lap, purring.

For the first few days, we tour the Amalfi Coast, Capri, and even Naples, where Gino plays silent bodyguard as my father unsuspectingly films. Later, in bed, Gino tells me that there were a number of thieves who had their sights set on my father's camcorder.

"I wish I could come with you to Venezia. It's not as dangerous as Napoli, but please be careful, *mi raccomando*."

Since I'm not yet confident enough to drive the *Seat* across Italy, my father and I take the train to Venice. We are both excited as the train crosses the causeway from Mestre to *La Serenissima* herself.

Venice is never tourist-free, but November is a good time to visit; there are cheap hotel rooms available, the crushing crowds of summer are gone, the chaos of *Carnevale* is still months away.

Venice has a calming effect on me. My father is so taken with everything this unique city has to offer, I don't even feel responsible for the tub-less bathroom we must share with other guests at the hotel. Somehow my worries seem unimportant in this bewitching labyrinth of alleys and canals, where art is everywhere and gondolas appear every time my father lifts his camera.

He is in his element, photographing me in all the typical spots: with the pigeons at Piazza San Marco, on the Ponte Rialto, in a gondola. I begin to feel as though I'm doing a fashion shoot.

We even order cappuccino to drink, sitting at a table in Piazza San Marco. It costs more than any coffee I've ever had, but I scarcely notice that we are breaking all the rules; it feels good to be a tourist. In the evenings, we dine in dim *trattorie* on Venetian specialties like *fegato alla Veneziana*, Venetian liver, and *farfalle con spinaci*, pasta bows with spinach.

It's only a two-day trip, but I've never spent so much time alone with my father. I tell him all about my life in Meta, about my job and my friends. I stay away from talk of the future, since such plans are not yet clear in my head.

Along with a few souvenirs and loads of photos and videotapes, my father and I carry a new relationship back to Sorrento. After all he has done for me, never asking anything in return, I have finally been able to be the giver, the leader, a responsible adult. And it was fun, not at all the chore I had imagined it might be.

On the way home, as misty vineyards slip by, my father reminisces wistfully of the days he travelled to South America on a twin-engine plane full of cattle. Blood runs thick, I think.

Two days before my father leaves, Adamo and Maria invite us to lunch. They are curious to meet a real *americano* of their own generation.

When we enter their courtyard, Maria sticks her head out of the kitchen window, squealing like a schoolgirl. "You're here! I'll be right down!" Then she bursts through the beaded fly screen at the bottom of the stairs, rushes up to my father, and shakes his hand, babbling all the while in dialect. My father forces an uncomfortable smile as she fusses us into the kitchen.

I smell fish. It is Friday; how could I have forgotten there would have to be fish? And not just fish, caught fresh by Adamo this morning, but also spaghetti *alle cozze*, with mussels scraped off the rocks by Maria herself. I could have told them in advance that my father does not like seafood, but now it is too late.

Adamo comes up from the orchard, all genuine smiles and welcoming handshakes. I see my father begin to relax in the presence of this man I secretly call grandfather. Adamo is ten years older than my father, but exudes the vitality of someone twenty years younger. His enthusiasm pulls us to the table, where we remain for two hours, as if under a spell. Wine will always loosen my father up, and Adamo plies him with glass after glass.

Adamo and Maria want to know about the climate in *America*, about food and farming and why my mother isn't here. I translate, we eat and drink; surprisingly, my father seems to like the food. We finish with espresso, *limoncello*, and chestnuts, more items my father would normally avoid, but by now I don't care, and my father must be of the same state of mind, for he accepts everything offered to him.

As we thank our hosts for a lovely time, Adamo loads us up with bags of lemons, oranges, wine, and olive oil. The weight of the bags, combined with our tipsy state, causes us to stagger in a zigzag fashion up the path to the car. I remark to my father that this is the way I always return home after a lunch with Adamo. He chuckles with a knowing smile.

Several months later, my mother arrives. She takes to Italy like a cat to a warm hearth. Whether she is basking on the beach, shopping for ceramics, or picnicking under pines, my mother is at once profoundly relaxed, yet more vibrant and alive than I have ever seen her.

If Italy was, for my father, Venice, red wine, and pizza, for my mother it is St. Francis, sweet springwater, and wild herbs. We take her to Assisi, where, never one to be satisfied with the surface story of myth, my mother searches for clues to the real St. Francis. She can feel his presence here, more so in the misty grey-green hills of olives and cypresses than in the tourist-trampled cathedral and alleyways, but all of Assisi is alluring. Steep streets hang with geraniums; the scent of fresh baked *biscotti* wafts into our small but comfy *pensione*.

We introduce my mother to Adamo's family; she adores their peaceful paradise of lemon groves and seascapes and feels at once the sacredness of Capo di Sorrento.

My mother insists she must travel to Naples to meet Gino's parents. I'm sure she will detest the smog and noise-filled city. What will she say to Signor and Signora Confalone? What could they possibly have in common?

Naples, to her, is an adventure, one she would not wish to live every day, but a place to experience a way of life she would never see back home. She hugs Gino's mother and father as if they are long-lost friends, not shy of the language barrier that always leaves me tongue-tied. They gesture and laugh, while Gino and I struggle to keep up with translations it seems they don't even need.

My mother appreciates Gino's mother's cooking, even though there is more salt and oil in this one meal than she would use in a year. It is a simply joyous occasion, and before we leave, we take a photo of the three of them hugging.

I am sorry my father never had this chance when he came to Italy. Unless pressured, Gino still keeps me and anything to do with me as much to himself as possible. My father, in his quiet accepting way, never questioned Gino.

Like Gino and me in Sardinia, my mother finds every day filled with new wonders, each one completely sublime in its own way. Assisi is the best, she says, or perhaps Capo di Sorrento, or the Greek ruins at Paestum. Perhaps it's Villa Cimbrone in Ravello, where she stands on a high terrace looking between statues down plunging cliffs to a sea so limpid the rocks are brilliantly visible, like icebergs below the surface.

After two weeks, my mother's spirit is irrevocably connected to all the places she has visited. Pulled by magic and the vibrations of history, she can hardly tear herself away. By the time she leaves, with promises to return, she is tanned and content, glowing inside and out with the essence of Italy.

Friends arrive, too, as friends do when one lives in a romantic dream world. But Italy lets me down.

I tell John and Cynthia that we'll be able to swim in April, so they excitedly pack light clothes and bathing suits, laughing up their short sleeves at the poor souls left behind in frigid Ontario. For their first week, the sun refuses to shine, and a damp chill prevails. Our apartment, delightfully cool in summer, seems cavernous and unpleasant. Our guests desire long hot showers each morning, which our pitiful bread-box water heater just can't provide.

I had so wanted them to admire our situation, but I have the distinct impression that they pity us instead. Cynthia is three months pregnant, suffering from morning, noon, and night sickness. We take them to Positano, expecting them to *ooh* and *ahh* at the views, but Cynthia buries her head between her knees, white fingers clutching John's arm.

The sun comes out during their second week, but there is no chance of a swim. It's too cold even for Gino. Of course, it's distinctly warmer than Ontario, but I had sold them a tropical holiday and failed to deliver.

Later on, another couple arrives, but even though it is midsummer, they prefer to sit in cafés drinking outrageously expensive glasses of wine while I swim alone from the rocks nearby.

"Poor Sheila," they lament. "She'll be crusted in sea salt for the rest of the day!"

Crusted! Never! I am kissed with salt! When I taste it on my lips, I remember how blessed I am to live close to the sea.

My friends seem uncharacteristically closed and negative. A few months later, I hear they are divorcing, and I wonder if that was the undercurrent I detected.

Italy is mine now, with all its merits and all its faults. Showing it to others clarifies my own perspective. I have taken this country to heart and shall never again be entirely separate from it.

Chapter 25

It's late fall and Signora Mosca and I are at odds. She wants me to teach Christmas carols to my students; I refuse. I simply cannot sing "Silent Night" or John Lennon's "And So This Is Christmas".

It's not that I don't want to sing. I have always admired those who can carry even the simplest of tunes, but it's a pure biological fact: my body doesn't produce music. It is a ridiculous standoff, but for us it is growing out of all proportion.

Signora Mosca knows that I am thinking of moving to Canada. She seems to take it personally, to resent that I will be leaving, that I will be forcing her to search for a replacement. She suspects I am giving private lessons on the side, which I am, but I've only stolen one student from her, at the student's request. This Christmas carol impasse gives her an excuse to vent her frustrations.

We discuss the issue daily for a week until she finally blows up, hurling accusations of selfishness and irresponsibility. Nothing she can say will change the truth of the matter: I can't teach what I don't know.

She finally agrees to make a cassette for me of her own voice that I can play for the class. This seems like a viable solution, but she holds it over me, refusing to speak to me, avoiding eye contact. The solution works well, but I become sick of hearing her voice. It's a relief when the school finally closes for the holidays.

Christmas is the greatest of Christian holidays; no one in southern Italy apologizes for this fact. I let myself be swept up in the fervour, and to my surprise, I enjoy it immensely.

All the women get together and bake for weeks. Seafood merchants rub their hands in glee as families try to outdo each other, respecting the centuries-old custom of serving enormous amounts and varieties of seafood on Christmas Eve, Christmas Day, and New Year's Eve. Every person who comes to our house brings a boxed *panettone* or *pandoro* cake. They begin to pile up on one corner of the table like flat-topped pyramids.

Gino is no great fan of tradition and always up for saving money, so when I suggest we commit the North American sin of regifting the cakes, he is immediately enthusiastic. I'm convinced others must be doing the same, but Gino thinks we are in the minority. Spending money lavishly and keeping up appearances is all part of the tradition. I scoff at the spending until I remember the frenzy of acquisition that occurs in North America at Christmastime.

Santa Claus is less prevalent here, perhaps because there are no shopping malls for him to hang around in, no tinsel-coated castles, no plush velvet chairs. Known in Italy as *Babbo Natale*, he might bring children a gift or two, but Italian tots wait for *La Befana*, a gruesome broom-riding witch who brings presents on Epiphany.

Despite the materialistic similarities between our two cultures, the true meaning of Christmas shines through much more brilliantly here. I have never been a huge proponent of Christianity, but I vow that if my future children are going to participate in all the magic of Christmas, I will make sure they understand its origins.

I have visions of building our own Neapolitan *presepe*, nativity scene, complete with moving parts, animals, and hillside inhabitants. I will visit the shops along Via San Gregorio Armeno to collect figurines—perhaps a water-bearing girl in silk robes and a ceramic camel complete with panniers full of fruit and wine. Out of moss-covered *sughero*, cork bark, we will construct green and brown foothills full of secret caves and simple dwellings, into which our visitors will peer to catch a glimpse of tiny glowing fireplaces. Outside, real water will gurgle in streams, cascading to tiny pools where it is conveyed back to the top of the scene by a hidden pump. Angels will hang on invisible thread, resplendent in gold and silver gowns, and yes, somewhere in there will be a small stable containing the holy family.

The remarkable thing about these scenes, and there are many grand ones to visit in Naples, is that Christ is not seen as separate, but as part of the natural world. His birth is represented as a miracle on Earth, for the benefit of all humankind.

Gino's family is full of sighs when we tell them we will be going to Abruzzo for Christmas. They are disappointed but not angry, assuming all Canadians must have an undeniable penchant for white Christmases. The real reason is that Gino doesn't want to share me with his family. Feast after family feast with all the requisite badgering and scrutinizing is more than he can bear.

We decide to take the train to Alfedena. Gino has heard of a mountain village called Villetta Barrea, not far from the station. He suggests we rent a chalet, where we can cuddle up together in front of a blazing fire while snow falls silently outside. I agree. Abruzzo is famous for its salamis and wines, so we add these to our tableau. A quick call to the tourist office in Villetta Barrea reassures us that there will be no problem finding accommodations once we arrive. We are eager for an adventure.

The train station at Alfedena lies at the foot of the mountains, with Villetta Barrea nestled somewhere over the other side. Alfedena isn't even a town, just a station in the middle of nowhere.

Stranded as we are, I am relieved to find balmy weather and not a speck of snow in sight.

We will be blessed with angels on this trip, and the first one shows up in the form of Signor Ponte. He acts as if there is nothing he would rather do than give us a lift over the mountains, he's going that way anyway, *nessun problema*. On the way, Signor Ponte tells us about his life, and we do the same. He drops us off at the tourist office in Villetta Barrea, gives us his business card, and makes us promise to call if we are ever back in the area. We promise sincerely.

The tourist office directs us to our next angel, Signora Luca, who has a chalet-type apartment for rent, complete with view of the valley and wood-burning stove.

We are settling in for a post lovemaking snack of wine and salami when Signora Luca knocks at the door.

"My husband and I will be hiking into the mountains with some *amici* tomorrow morning. Our destination is a cave that hides a hidden spring. We make this *pellegrinaggio* every Christmas Eve. Would you like to join us?"

We don't hesitate. "We'd love to!"

"*Benissimo*. Pack a lunch. It will take most of the day to get there and back."

During the hike through misty air and golden chestnut leaves, we take deep breaths, fuelling our bodies with heady earth scents. Every once in a while, we cross a burbling stream that must surely be the issue of our destination. The walk is long but not strenuous. The last bit is a steep climb over rocky terrain, but then the mouth of the cave is above us, welcoming us. The headwaters bubble out of a fissure in the back wall, surging over the cave's lip to cascade down the rocks.

We climb inside; there is plenty of space for the six of us. After we drink from the spring, Signor Luca pulls a bottle of champagne from his pack. We solemnly toast the true spirit of Christmas, of angels and blessings. The bubbles of the champagne become one with the gurgle of the spring, and we are instantly giddy, anointing ourselves with this purest of waters. Infused with rapture, we emerge joyfully into the afternoon.

The spirit of the cave, the water, the chestnuts—this is my natural religion. I feel it quickening now within me. Gino feels it. The others feel it. It is the reason they make the pilgrimage every year to drink at this eternal fountain of nature.

The walk back is like floating on mist. Evening is setting in when we arrive effortlessly back in the village. Christmas lights welcome us to a scene from an Italian *presepe*. We bid *buon natale* to our companions and retire to our chalet. As night falls, so do large flakes of snow. They drift past the dark window, illuminated by our fire.

Snow at Christmas has always been magical, but this snow is special. It seems to be the risen springwater descending in another form to blanket the sacred earth. We watch, mesmerized by the constant whirl of flakes and the flickering warmth of the fire. Our eyes begin to droop; we make our way to the bedroom, where we snuggle together and sleep the blissful slumber of the truly serene.

The next morning we step out into deep snow, something all too familiar to me. Something Gino has never done before. Peaked chalet roofs hang with snow icing. The lake below shimmers like crinkly foil, not ice but icy cold.

I am struck by the diversity of Italy. This Alpine village is just as picturesque as the Amalfi coast, but entirely different. Italy seems to be divided into two types of people—those who prefer to vacation by the sea and those who prefer to vacation in the mountains. The choice isn't always to do with where one lives, for even in Sorrento, entire class discussions can centre around this topic. Gino's allegiance lies with the sea, but he is smitten by this winter wonderland.

The snow begins to melt as the sun rises higher, and we walk the lake trail without jackets. I like this kind of winter, one that bestows splendid shining moments, then melts into jaunty rivulets.

We spend New Year's Eve at home in Meta, walking to the beach to watch the display of fireworks, but I am so terrorized by the rockets whizzing past my head, fizzing in the sand near my feet, crashing onto the breakwater, that we decide to return home before midnight.

"This is *niente*," says Gino. "Napoli goes absolutely mad on New Year's Eve. It's the ultimate excuse to let loose with noise and fire."

I am relieved to be within our twelve-inch-thick stone walls; our apartment is a veritable bomb shelter.

Later, during a quick celebratory call to Naples, we hear that Ettore's new car, parked outside his building, has been blown up by a stray firework that became lodged underneath.

New Year's Day, by contrast, is utterly silent. Nothing stirs, save spent firecrackers shifting on the cobblestones and rustling in the orange trees. We drive to Positano, but everything there is closed tight. We have the distinct impression that families are spending a quiet day together. I wonder if Gino wishes, just a little, to be with his. I am melancholy, longing for mine.

The new year has always been a difficult time for me, a time when I feel obliged to review my life and make plans for the future. "No more coasting along," the new year says. "Time to get serious."

Where will this year take us? We talk it over on the deserted beach in Positano. Marriage? A move to Canada? Is it time to take these big steps? I've had an idea in my mind for a while, and now seems like a good time to broach it with Gino.

"We could import gloves to Canada and sell them there. We could set up a kiosk in a shopping centre in Toronto or Ottawa or Kingston and see how it goes. It would be seasonal work, but we could make enough money during the winter season to take it easy the rest of the year. Or, if business started slowly, I could find a teaching job. What if we could live half the year in Canada and half the year in Italy?" I ramble on.

Gino is willing to indulge me, and over the next weeks we discuss details and research possibilities. The Chambers of Commerce in Toronto, Ottawa, and Kingston fax us information about shopping centres. The shopping centre administrators send us information about rents and policies.

"Canada is so organized!" exclaims Gino.

Even I am amazed. We just have to contact the right government office, and the next thing we know, a package of documents as thick as a phone book arrives. All our questions about setting up a small business in Canada are answered.

Gino decides to put in extra hours at the factory, cutting velvet and microfibre himself. Then he pays the seamstresses out of his own pocket, slowly stockpiling pair after pair of gloves. He stores them in huge boxes in the factory basement, ready to ship to Canada.

When I'm available, I help too. I'm fascinated by the monstrous rolls of fabric in brilliant colours, soft colours, natural colours. I try to imagine which ones would sell best in Canada. For the first time in my life, I research fashion trends.

I watch Gino roll out giant swathes of fabric on the cutting table, where he slices them with a saw made just for this purpose. Then he chops the stacked layers into glove shapes with the ancient *pressa* that has been used by his family for generations. We will order a selection of leather gloves as well, from one of Gino's contacts *di fiducia*. The gloves are elegant works of art, which every Canadian will be lining up to buy.

"Imagine the Christmas season!" I gush, dreaming of dollar signs. "What could be a more perfect gift than a pair of Italian gloves? We'll have trouble keeping enough in stock! We could sell wholesale, too. All we have to do is tour around, show samples; any shop would beg to have our gloves!"

Whether this risky, expensive venture is headed for success or failure, we, ourselves, are on an unstoppable trajectory towards Canada.

Chapter 26

Throughout the next months, the idea of marriage grows in our hearts. There is no getting down on bended knee, no engagement ring. It is simply a part of the life path we are travelling together, an exquisite flower we are compelled to collect along the way. Because of this simple, natural interpretation, we decide to marry in Canada, at my parents' house with just a few friends present.

Gino's mother is torn between distress and relief. Finally, after two years of living in sin, we will become husband and wife, but we will not bow to Italian tradition. (No church! No *bomboniere*! The bride in a mini-dress!) She and Gino's father are afraid to fly, so their participation will be limited to wiring flowers and telephoning *auguri*, best wishes, on the day. They know that after the honeymoon, we will return to live in Italy for another year, but they see this wedding as leading inevitably towards the loss of their son to the other side of the ocean.

Gino discourages his brothers and sisters from making the expensive trip. "We'll celebrate once we get back to Italia," he promises.

On the day itself, a sweltering thirty-first of August, the flowers are loudly congratulatory, but the phone call is more of a warning.

"Heed my words," says my mother-in-law from across the ocean. "Take good care of my son." And although it is not spoken aloud, I hear the *or else* in her voice.

At first, I'm not sure how to answer, but then it becomes clear to me that the only thing I can do is reassure her. She deserves this small gift. Her words are not so much a warning as a plea.

For our honeymoon, we fly to Alberta, rent a car, and drive through the Rocky Mountains to British Columbia. We visit the ice fields and walk on a ten-thousand-year-old glacier. In Jasper, we meet elk in the streets. On Vancouver Island, we camp in an old-growth forest and barbecue a whole salmon, fresh off the boat. This is Canada at its best. We both feel focused, ready to give in to the pull of our future.

Chapter 27

It is mid-September when we return to Italy, relieved to find that our apartment remains as we left it. Anxious to spend time with our friends, we arrange a day at the beach with Ciro and Arianna. Ciro drives us to Nerano, on the other side of the peninsula. We park and walk down wooden steps to a pebbly beach.

Ciro takes his shirt off and settles on the blanket Arianna has brought. He is strikingly pale-skinned for one of Mediterranean blood. Arianna remains fully clothed in black and white silk pants, long-sleeved matching blouse, and giant sun hat. The whole elegant ensemble is topped off with gold jewellery: a complete set of matching earrings, bracelets, and necklace. She takes off her shoes and stands close to the water, letting small waves wash over her toes. She clearly has no intention of going any further.

Gino inflates the air mattress, chatting with Ciro between breaths. He likes to let the sun warm his body first. Then he will take a long, leaping run through the shallows, curve his body into a dive, and butterfly into the deeps.

I strip to my bikini and wade straight out to waist level. I wear plastic sandals since the rocks underfoot can be sharp. I plunge down underwater, but instead of the refreshing rush I expect, every nerve in my left arm is suddenly screaming pain signals to my brain. I break the surface, gasping.

I am surrounded by jellyfish, their semitransparent bodies pumping and fluttering all around me, tentacles of unknown length invisible to my eye. I force myself to stand still while shrieking for Gino, who grabs the air mattress and paddles out to me. I climb on board, and we float above the minefield, the surge of the sea carrying us to shore.

A small crowd gathers to inspect my stinging wound. There are many suggestions, but the main consensus seems to be that I should apply tomato slices to the red welt that travels up the inside of my arm. Arianna dissects our sandwiches, and I rest against Gino while she applies tomatoes to my skin. I am relieved to find that it helps. Everyone has moved away from the water's edge as jellyfish begin to wash up on shore.

"This happens," says Ciro. "There won't be any jellyfish at all for days, and then they catch a *corrente* and travel inland in huge masses."

Arianna is visibly repulsed and says she can't wait to get in the car and go home. We eat our picnic first: *prosciutto* and mozzarella sandwiches minus the tomatoes. I am restored, only a small tingle of irritation remaining. Gino is undaunted.

"We'll be more careful next time and have a look first with the mask."

"You're crazy," says Arianna as she replaces her gold leather sandals. "Sharp rocks, jellyfish, salt that dries on your skin…. I don't know how you can bear it!"

Arianna talks of food on the way home. "Have you ever tried pizza with *rugola?*" she asks me.

"What's *rugola?*"

"It's that herb right there," she says, pointing to the side of the road. "Ciro! Stop the car!" He pulls over, and Arianna hops out to gather a handful of herbs. "Try this."

I chew a leaf, crisp and spicy. It's delicious, but I have trouble imagining it on pizza.

"You will love it," says Ciro. "Tomorrow we will have dinner at *da Salvatore*, and you can try."

The answering machine takes Ciro's call as usual while we are lying in bed late on Sunday morning. When Gino phones him back around noon, Ciro is indignant.

"Go ahead and waste your day however you want. We'll meet you at seven o'clock at *da Salvatore* in Colli di Fontanelle."

"He's just jealous," laughs Gino, wiping the last of the *biscotti* crumbs from the table. He picks up my canvas bag and packs it with our masks, flippers, towels, and a change of bathing suits, while I prepare sandwiches for lunch and put them in Gino's day pack. Then we're off to Conca dei Marini for a day of snorkelling and sunbathing.

After a full day at the beach, a late afternoon shower, nap, and languorous session of lovemaking, we are twenty minutes late for our dinner date.

"Good evening, *spagnoli!*" shouts Ciro from across the restaurant.

He calls us "Spanish" in order to imply that we spend all our time sleeping. He likes to joke about Spain, and as we seat ourselves at the table, he starts to mock the wine and the food of Arianna's country.

Arianna cuts him off, reminding him how she had to drag him away from every bar they encountered on their last visit to Bilbao. "You ate so many tapas and drank so much wine, I thought you would explode!"

"Well, yes," he admits, "There is a sausage called *chorizo*, which is delectable. I drank the wine from pure thirst, though."

"You loved more than the *chorizo*, and you know it," remarks Arianna.

Having met his match, Ciro turns to me.

"At least the *spagnoli* don't drink themselves stupid on vodka and whiskey like people in Canada and those other godforsaken northern countries."

Ciro's fondness of a good argument goes unrequited. Gino knows I'm not in the mood, so he changes the subject.

"What do you recommend, Ciro? Have you tried the *parmigiana di zucchini*?"

Ciro is distracted, and I pick up my menu. Arianna, Gino, and I order pizza with *rugola*. It is different from what I imagined, with the herb sprinkled fresh on top, not baked along with the other ingredients. I crunch its green spiciness, mixing flavours of creamy mozzarella, fresh tomato sauce, and garlic in my mouth.

Gino, in typical fashion, takes a monstrous bite, rolling his eyes in ecstasy. "*Delizioso*," he murmurs, olive oil dripping from his chin.

We are hooked. Never again will we return empty-handed from our hikes along mountain trails. As we learn more and more about the wild herbs available, even our trips to Positano will become scavenger hunts as we discover arugula, fennel, and other edible plants growing alongside the steps that once seemed overgrown with weeds. We carry home our *verdure* in plastic bags and cook up fragrant *frittate*, complimenting ourselves on our delicious frugality.

"Try this," urges Ciro, brandishing a forkful of marinated eggplant.

"*Allora*, it's good," Gino begins, "but...."

I know what he's going to say. No one, not even Salvatore, could possibly make marinated eggplant as well as Gino's mother. I call her *La Regina delle Melanzane*, the Eggplant Queen. Whether she marinates it, grills it, bakes it into *parmigiana*, or chops it into *funghetti*, she never fails to astound with the delectability of her creations.

I have tried to copy her recipes; Gino is politely appreciative of my efforts, but eventually I give up, accepting instead with gratitude the aluminum take-out containers Mamma sends home every once in a while.

At nine o'clock, Gino suggests we go to Gelateria Gabriele in Vico Equense for dessert. Ciro is skeptical that we, outsiders from Naples and Canada, could possibly know of a place worth visiting that he himself has not already discovered.

Gino found Gabriele's during a train strike when he was forced to get off at Vico Equense, two stops before Meta. He has since made several trips on special occasions to buy homemade *delizie al limone*, which Gabriele himself places on a tray, wrapping it with monogrammed paper and ribbon. *Delizie al limone* are not ice cream, but rather light cakes covered and layered with fresh lemon cream. Served chilled to almost freezing, there is no more refreshingly calorific way to top off a meal. Ciro takes a bite, then puts his arm around Gino. "You've surprised me again," he says.

How easy it is to live simply here. People in Canada might consider us desperately poor because we have no living room, no bathtub, a beat-up car. But we are surrounded by a Mediterranean paradise—who cares about all the rest?

We eat cheaply, too. What could be better than spaghetti with mussels we have pried from the rocks ourselves or a *frittata* made with fresh fennel fronds we have picked on a sun-drenched hill facing Capri? (Ciro says the sweetest herbs will always be found facing in this direction. Nothing to do with sun exposure, but simply for the pure joy of growing face-to-face with such *splendore*).

We get our *provola* cheese, both regular and *affumicata*, smoked, from Rafaele, a pasty vampire-type who rarely sees the light of day, holed up as he is in his dank *caseficio*. Sometimes we make a meal of thickly sliced rounds of cheese melted over the fire between two lemon leaves.

Adamo provides us with an endless supply of lemons, chestnuts, wine, and olive oil.

Our oregano is grown on Mount Vesuvius by a wrinkled raisin of a man. He comes into town on his bicycle, towing a wooden cart full of dried herbs tied in bunches. If we want three thousand lire worth, he will inevitably push us to spend five thousand since, after all, he has made such a long trip and his product is of unmatched quality.

We usually collect our mussels during snorkelling expeditions along the Amalfi Coast, but one day, Adamo's wife, Maria, offers to show me where they grow at Capo.

"We must go early in the *mattina*, before the hydrofoils to Capri start up in full force," she says. "The *scia* they make will toss you against the sharp rocks."

The next morning, buckets and kitchen knives in hand, we walk down the ancient cobbled path to the sea, past Adamo's usual bathing spot near Queen Giovanna's baths, and across a wooden walkway to more rocks. We lower ourselves into the sea, smooth and calm at this hour. Thousands of mussels cling to the jagged rocks. We fill one bucket and half of another before the first hydrofoil of the day comes into view around the headland.

"*Esci dall'acqua,*" urges Maria, and I scramble up out of the sea just before the heavy wake crashes against the shore.

We return to Maria's kitchen, where Adamo has a tray of home-preserved anchovies on bread waiting for us. I'm ravenous, and the anchovies, drenched in garlic-scented olive oil, are delicious. For me, this is breakfast. For Adamo, it is a midmorning snack, even though it is only nine o'clock.

Adamo organizes his day like this: up at four to fish or tend the chickens, rabbits, and the pig I call "sausage" since this is the form in which I met his predecessor. Breakfast at six, then more chores including mending grape trellises and collecting firewood. Swim from ten o'clock to one o'clock, lunch, siesta. The afternoon chores are dictated by the seasons: sorting olives for transport to the *frantoio*, peeling lemons for *limoncello*, making wine from the *grappoli* that hang from trellises built among the lemon trees.

Maria will spend the rest of her morning shucking the pail of mussels to make sauce for her family of six. Not so used to hard labour, I will take a much smaller quantity home, steam them open, then throw them, shells and all, into a light tomato sauce. We will deal with them individually as we eat, slurping each juicy morsel from its shell.

Adamo is happy to take a break from his schedule to grill me about Gino's intentions, about my own hopes and dreams for the future. When we are finished with the usual grandfatherly business, he hands me a bag full of *limoni di pane*, lemons the size of grapefruit. "Show these to Gino," he says. "He'll know what to do with them."

When Gino arrives home, he gives me a quick kiss, then heads straight for the fruit on the table. "Ooh, *limoni di pane!*" he cries, grabbing one while simultaneously fumbling in the drawer for a knife. "Taste this!" He slices a wedge, thick with pith.

"Yuck," I think before I bite, but when I do, I discover yet another delectable taste of Italy.

One Saturday, I glance out the window above the stove to see Signor De Falco in the garden picking fava beans. It's late morning, and we have just finished breakfast.

"We'd better refill the *moka* in case he comes in," says Gino.

I empty out the grounds and hand the pot to Gino. I will not make espresso for anyone except us. Only a Neapolitan can make coffee for another Neapolitan. A Milanese won't make it right, so how can you expect someone who comes from the other side of the ocean, who once enjoyed the dreaded *caffè americano*, to appreciate, let alone prepare a decent cup of espresso?

Italians can't agree amongst themselves on the proper method. Opinion varies wildly around whether the coffee grounds should be packed firmly or loosely, whether the water should reach the bottom of the valve or the middle of the valve, whether sugar should be added right into the pot or after, into the cups. How full should the cups be? Certainly nowhere near the top.

173

But halfway? One-third? Should the pot stay on the stove until it has sputtered its last breath, or be removed from the burner while still bubbling madly, steam shooting out of the valve? I am not qualified to make these decisions, so I'm happy to have Gino take over.

Sure enough, Signor De Falco appears at the door, a bag of *fave* in hand. "These are for you, Signora," he says, handing the beans to me.

I have no idea what to do with fresh fava beans, but I thank him and invite him in. Gino offers what to me seems an embarrassingly small amount of coffee, not exactly a thimbleful, but close.

Signor De Falco downs it in one gulp, nodding approvingly. "*Vado di fretta*, I'm in a hurry," he says. "*Grazie del caffè.* Enjoy your *fave.*"

Gino closes the door behind the landlord, and I pick up a bright green pod, as long as my forearm. "What do we do with these?"

"You can cook them, but the best way is to eat them raw, at the end of a meal to aid digestion, or with salami as an *antipasto.*" Gino opens a pod, handing me the large oval beans from the inside. He pops one into his mouth. "Mmm, wonderful."

I chew one myself, trying hard to like it, but the bitter, irony flavour is more like medicine, like something my mother might make me eat just because it's good for me.

"They're full of *vitamine*," Gino says, munching happily on his second handful.

"Hmm, yes. They must be an acquired taste."

Gino has no idea what this means. All children in Italy are brought up on rapini, chard, fennel, beans, cabbage. There's no forcing them to eat vegetables. They just do, and they like them. This amazes me. Any children I knew back home had to be bribed or punished into finishing their vegetables. It's almost as though an Italian's tastes are completely formed from childhood. There is no "acquiring." Sure, children eat cookies for breakfast, but they eat a heaping plate of rice and beans for lunch, fish and broccoli for dinner, all prepared lovingly by Mamma or Nonna from the freshest ingredients.

According to Gino, his mother makes the best *pizze con scarole*. He has told me about this legendary dish, and on my next visit, I am to try it. It doesn't look at all like pizza, more like a thick bread stuffed with escarole, a bitter cousin of lettuce that, in my opinion, should only be eaten in small quantities, preferably buried under other more delicate greens.

But here I am in his mother's kitchen, and I don't want to disappoint. I will need to eat a suitable quantity in order to convince her that I'm not just pretending to like it. Gino and his mother watch as I take a bite of the enormous slab placed in front of me.

The dough is like *focaccia*; it tastes of fresh-ground flour and olive oil. The escarole in the centre, I'm delighted to find, has been cooked with garlic and olive oil to minimize the bitterness. I'm sold.

I realize how lucky Italian children are; their mothers know how to make things taste good. Imagine presenting North American children with fried zucchini flowers, pasta with squash or cabbage, boiled tripe, marinated octopus; a menu like this would send them screaming to their rooms.

I want to be able to cook like an Italian. Gino has the magic touch. He can throw a pot of rice and cabbage together and have it turn into a delectable meal I can't stop eating. The secret seems to be in the olive oil, the garlic, the pecorino cheese. Why doesn't it taste the same when I make it? It must be the quantities, for one thing. I'm afraid to use a *pugno*, handful, of salt in anything. To me, more than a tablespoon of oil is too much. Italians don't even bother with spoons, moving directly into portions of a litre. A *decilitro* of olive oil is usually a good starting point for any Neapolitan dish. The amount of olive oil Gino's family uses astounds me. They cook with it, dress salads with it, preserve everything from anchovies to eggplant in it.

In the south, you will be hard-pressed to find butter in the kitchen. Since *uno toast* is actually a sandwich grilled in oil, why would you need it? Why would you put butter on bread? It would simply hinder the soaking up of all the surrounding flavours. Buttery sauces are not popular; a simple *aglio e olio*, garlic and oil base will do for just about everything. And tomatoes. Lots and lots of tomatoes.

Lack of wood and knowledge have kept us from trying our pizza oven. You make a fire in it, it has to get really hot, but then what? We don't know how to make dough, how long to bake it, how to control the fire so the pizza doesn't go up in flames.

Luckily, Lisa's boyfriend, Dario, used to be a *pizzaiolo*, pizza chef. "*Guarda che bello*, what a beauty!" he exclaims at the sight of our oven. He works now as a tour guide and is thrilled to have the opportunity to practice his neglected art.

Dario drops off wood the day before: hard cherry and olive, collected from a farmer. Dario and Lisa arrive at six o'clock, laden with bags full of pizza dough, chopped mozzarella, *San Marzano* tomatoes, and basil. Expertly, Dario tends the fire we have already started; a blasting heat begins to emanate from the arched oven doorway. He assures us it will soon reach the required six hundred degrees Celsius, then proceeds to wreak havoc in my gleaming white-tiled kitchen.

By the time he has finished making six large rectangular pizzas, there is a dusting of flour and ash over everything, including the walls. Below the oven, there is a puddle of black water, dripped from the twig broom he has been using to sweep embers out of the way. The odd stray tomato squelches underfoot.

I decide to ignore the mess and deal with cleanup in the morning. I forget all about the disaster in my kitchen when I bite into the best pizza I have ever tasted. The dough is soft and light, the toppings simply heaven, and every mouthful has that distinctive flavour only a wood-burning oven can provide. We eat our fill, drink two bottles of wine, finish off with icy *limoncello*, then pack the rest of the pizza to eat on the beach in Positano the next day.

"It will taste even better by then," says Dario.

I doubt anything could taste better than this, but I am learning that with food, as with everything else in Italy, I must keep an open mind.

Chapter 28

One day, while I'm teaching a class at Language World, the room tilts. The motion is quick, almost imperceptible, like the nudge of a well-maintained elevator. Before I understand what's happening, it's over.

There is a split second of silence before the students all start talking at once, joking nervously and wanting to know my reaction to the earthquake. I am stunned at first, then exhilarated. Yes, exhilarated. The living planet has shifted below me, instantly altering my perspective and connecting me to the infinite cycle of geological creation and destruction.

Most of my students don't share my enthusiasm. Neither, apparently, does Signora Mosca, who has immediately raced down the stairs and out into the square. She and most of my students had lived through the much larger earthquake of 1980. It lasted a terrifying ninety seconds and caused widespread devastation.

This region of Italy has had its share of natural disasters. The Sorrentine Peninsula has been spared from the worst, but places less than thirty miles away like Pompeii and Herculaneum attest to monumental misfortunes. These cities were buried under lava and volcanic ash when Vesuvius erupted in 79 AD and have been unearthed over the last few hundred years to reveal a civilization frozen in time.

Almost a million people live around the periphery of Mount Vesuvius, despite a government initiative offering large sums of money for relocation.

"Why do people continue to build houses on an active volcano?" I wonder.

"Because it's cheap," Gino replies. "Property *prezzi* elsewhere are so high, the government *incentivo* amounts to about a tenth of what families need to start over. Besides, *Vesuvio* hasn't erupted in many years. People are forgetting."

I feel there must be more to it, for how can you argue scientific probabilities with Neapolitans, a people proud to be counted among the contrary believers of the world? Flowery offerings grease the palms of saints, or at least their likenesses, installed conveniently into street-side niches like pay phones with a direct line to God.

Did a statue of San Gennaro mysteriously topple over in the night? There will be a run on the lottery number nineteen because it corresponds to this saint in *La Smorfia*, a guide to Neapolitan lottery numbers and their symbols. Nineteen doesn't come up? Well, you should have played one and nine separately since San Gennaro split in two when he hit the ground. There is always a higher power at work. Communicate effectively with this power, divine its methods, and all will be well. Connections are everything.

The power I wish to communicate with lies not only in the heavens, but also under my feet. In Naples, shrouds of chaos and human growth cover the natural past. I miss the immense, almost untouched face of the Canadian wilderness. I long to walk for hours in a forest without seeing or hearing another human being.

Even on our relatively peaceful peninsula, not one stone remains unturned. Every possible space has been exploited for growing olives, lemons, or grapes. On solitary walks, across seemingly deserted mountains, I hear the shrill cries of a goatherd or the startling report of a gun.

The earthquake has awakened a primal desire within me. My natural core yearns to experience, at a deeper level, this power that is somehow connected to the forests of Canada and yet so different from anything I have known before.

Gino understands my need. One chilly day in February, he takes me to Pozzuoli, just north of Naples, to visit the Solfatara. It is a brimstone-scented place where Mother Earth's heart beats close to the surface, where her breath steams and mud-blood bubbles.

The Solfatara is an active caldera that remains in a sort of perpetual slow-motion eruption. Back in the early 80s, an area including most of the town of Pozzuoli was uplifted, in places to a height of six feet. Homes were destroyed and people forced to relocate, but Pozzuolians, like their neighbours in Naples, maintain a fatalistic optimism.

I am not entirely afraid since we have paid an admission to enter this no-man's-land. It is a natural attraction, like Yosemite's geysers, supposedly safe if you follow the rules and stay away from the roped-off areas.

We have the place to ourselves, and as I step out into the sulphurous valley, I have the strange sensation of walking on another planet, while at the same time feeling closer to the Earth than ever before. We are careful not to step in the pools of boiling mud or on the *fumaroli*, holes out of which vapour hisses.

"According to *legenda*," says Gino, "this is where the Greeks first conceived their idea of hell."

I find the place eerie, but strangely welcoming. A half-ruined Roman sauna beckons to us, and we crouch inside, breathing deeply, letting the thick warmth invade our lungs and bodies. We come out feeling drugged. I crave more.

The next weekend, we continue my quest. A bus takes us partway up Vesuvius, then we walk. The side of the crater is bare rubble. Nothing grows in this sun-scorched environment, and I am glad there is a fresh winter breeze. Eight hundred feet above the sea, we have a grand panorama of the Bay of Naples. The islands of Procida, Ischia, and Capri rise from the azure expanse like prehistoric sea creatures.

We approach the edge of the caldera and peer into the mouth of Vesuvius, a pit full of rocks, steam, and garbage. Then we look the other way, down towards Pompeii. Between the crater and the excavation site, there is just us and a couple of miles of volcanic scree. The sun paints our shadows on the vapour, causing our image to shimmer inside the crater.

Somewhere far below our feet, the Earth's skeleton is contorting; the African plate is slowly pushing itself beneath the Eurasian plate, causing the Mediterranean basin to shrink, Vesuvius to remain active, and Pozzuoli to rise. How can we not feel this with our whole being? We stand here insolently, out of touch with our real beginnings. I shift pebbles of solidified magma under the soles of my shoes. Some trickle down the slope towards distant terraces heavily cultivated with broccoli, lettuce, anise, citrus fruit, and flowers.

"Volcanic soil is the most fertile on the planet." says Gino.

I'm about to say how ironic it is that such a violent force produces vibrant new life, but then I realize that it has nothing to do with irony. It is simply the way nature works, forever creating and consuming and creating again. I pick up a pebble and hold it in the palm of my hand. It is rough and cool, but I can feel an energy within it that was once sultry and smooth as blood.

The following weekend, we take the train to Pompeii. I had already been here during my early days as a culture-blind tourist. Ignoring the modern city, I had made a beeline for the excavations. But now my eyes are opening to the layers of Italy. I see that Pompeii is traffic jams and tramways, language schools and supermarkets, hospitals and banks. And six hundred thousand people, who go about their business, seemingly as oblivious to the threat of Vesuvius as those who lived and died here in 79 AD.

Gino's sister, Ornella, will be married at Our Lady of Pompeii, a sacred place where pilgrims flock to give thanks for a cure or to pray for benediction. All of Gino's family will be here. And I will attend, struggling in high heels on the cobbled streets, understanding little of the lengthy ceremony, admiring instead the grand interior of the massive church. How many of us will notice Vesuvius that day? Certainly not Ornella, who will be too busy worrying about the dirt on her hemline and the smooth running of the impending twelve-course meal. Like most Italian brides, she has spent the last twelve months shopping, planning, and agonizing over each detail. The stress of arguing daily with her mother and future in-laws about such minutiae as whether the marinated clams should be served before or after the grilled octopus will have caused her to lose weight. This wedding is the grand culmination of all that sweat and anguish; Vesuvius is only an afterthought, if that.

Revisiting the excavations, I am drawn, not to the mosaics, temples, and shops, but to the suffocated bodies, eerie prostrate forms preserved forever in volcanic ash. Flesh is gone, but a presence remains, laid bare for even the chaos-weary to perceive. What could be a more striking reminder of nature's power?

Chapter 29

Packing for our move to Canada is a painful chore. We sort through our things, deciding what to leave in storage at Gino's parents' place. Our snorkelling gear, dinghy, extra towels, bulky bathrobes, a silver miniskirt from Arianna that I never wore, all go into large cardboard boxes. We have no furniture, no pots and pans, no dishes. Just the tiny *moka* and a very good corkscrew Costantino gave me.

While we sort and pack, Tigrotto looks expectantly at his new cat carrier, recently bought at a pet store in Naples by an unhesitating Gino. Tigrotto has no idea of the life that awaits him in Canada. Gino and I will probably find a small city apartment, so Tigrotto will live with my parents in the country. He will find chipmunks instead of lizards, trees of a type he has never climbed, snowflakes that seem like fun to chase until they pile up so high he will only be able to follow my father's footsteps, bounding from one deep print to the next. Of an evening, he will curl up by the fire or on my father's lap, dreaming perhaps of his kittenhood across the ocean. I look at him now, nestled in the same small basket he had when I first brought him home. Instead of the tiny mite who once peered nervously over the edge of the basket, his plush body now overflows the sides like well-risen bread.

Gino, too, has no real idea of what life in Canada will offer. How hard it must be for him to pack up his life and follow me. After three years in Italy, I know it's not easy to make such a monumental change. But he is focused on new possibilities, on starting a family and a business. And I'm sure he sees moving as an escape—from the factory, which has claimed his family for too many years, and from that same prying, privacy-less family that he loves but will perhaps love more from a distance.

He will certainly miss the sea, the gentle climate, his language, his friends. He will love the open spaces, the freedom, and the forests (although not the many biting and stinging insects within). Every winter, blinding snowstorms and freezing rain will likely make him want to hightail it back to Naples. Canada will be a place of fewer excitements, less history, and bland food, but I hope Gino will see it as a good, safe place to raise a family. When I express my dream of living part-time in both countries, he replies, "*vedremo*, we'll see," as if, perhaps, my dreams are flying too fast, too far, and it's time to settle down.

My marriage to Gino is the only commitment I have felt comfortable with; in the past, any relationship that tied me down was mercilessly cast aside. I had two 'real' jobs after university: one teaching, one as an office manager. Within days of accepting the positions, all I could do was plan my escape, devising elaborate excuses for why I suddenly desired to tear my contract to shreds. Waitressing jobs were perfect for me, easy come, easy go. A friend once insisted I should do bigger and better things with my life. What could be better, I scoffed, than doing exactly as I pleased?

Now I struggle with the load of responsibility the move bestows upon me. What if Gino hates Canada? What if he pines for his homeland, unable to function in a new culture? His disillusionment will be my fault, and I will simply expire under the sheer weight of remorse. In weak moments, I wonder if we might not better stick to Italy and raise a family here, where Gino would be the one to take the heat for all his country's shortcomings.

I try to figure out an alternative plan for the two of us. We can always come back to Italy if we change our minds. After all, people have raised families here for centuries. But then I think of a Canadian friend whose father finally committed suicide after switching countries four times, always unhappy with both Canada and his homeland.

I remember Adamo's words and hope Gino will be one of the truly content immigrants. The wondering exhausts me, and at night I fall asleep wishing I could dream our future and know it now in every detail.

We drive to Capo di Sorrento one last time and say good-bye to the magical place where we first met. Walking hand in hand with Gino down the path to the sea, I notice how the cobbles are now cupped comfortably under my soles. This path is no smoother than it was when I first came, but it is familiar, like the many places and people that were once entirely unknown to me.

The sea is calm and peaceful. I breathe its salty scent deep into my lungs; Gino does the same. There are a few tourists enjoying the sun on the rocks. A proprietary pride wells up within me, and I feel as though I should tell them, "This is a sacred place; treat it well." We take one last breath of sea air, one last look across the Gulf towards Capri, then turn and walk up the path to Adamo's green gate.

Adamo is waiting in his courtyard under the lemon trees. "Good luck in America," he says, solemnly shaking Gino's hand. And then, holding his gaze, gripping harder, "*Mi raccomando,* take good care of my girl." Adamo and I hug tightly, charging our connection so it will last over time and oceans. "Take this with you," he says, handing me a parcel full of his own lifeblood: chestnuts, lemons, olive oil, wine. We thank him and take it, though we're not sure how we'll get it past Customs.

We stop in Piano to say good-bye to Arianna, Ciro, Dario,

and Lisa. Arianna says she will visit us as soon as possible. "You are so lucky to be going home."

Ciro is skeptical of the move. He can't believe anyone would want to leave the peninsula. He jokes with Gino, but his concern comes through. "Try not to resort to drinking vodka to keep warm," he says, giving Gino the kind of hug only Italian men can give.

Dario and Lisa wish us luck and offer to drive us to the airport.

"*Grazie*, but no," Gino says. "We will be spending the day in Napoli with my family before we leave."

We make several trips to Naples in the *Seat*. Once the final load is in the trunk and Tigrotto in his carrier, we lock the door to our apartment for the last time. I cry. I have loved this place like no other. I have been loved here like never before. The towns on the way to Naples look less squalid, the volcano less threatening. The city itself seems to welcome us. I imagine I hear it declare to Gino, "I am part of you."

My heart breaks when we say good-bye to Gino's family. Struggling to hold back sobs, his mother makes the sign of the cross, her silent blessing to us. His brother Roberto drives us to the airport. I can tell there is too much in his heart to express. He says simply, "*Mi raccomando*, take care of yourselves."

The sun beats down on the tarmac as we cross to the plane and board. We are silent, lost in our own thoughts. When the plane takes off, we lean into each other, watching the brilliance of the Gulf of Naples fade to less than blue.

Epilogue

We live in Canada now. Our children are growing up Canadian. Gino works hard, in the way of new immigrants who take nothing for granted. The retail glove business fell disastrously by the wayside, giving way to the much more realistic world of wholesale. Each year, Gino masterfully negotiates orders, shipments, and Canada Customs. His English has improved immensely, through sheer will and immersion. My heart is full of pride and relief.

He has driven in freezing rain and suffered thousands of mosquito bites. He has shovelled hundreds of feet of snow from the driveway and cut miles of grass with a push mower. He makes pizza, bread, and pasta while listening to his favourite Italian songs on the stereo. We swim in lakes instead of the sea, spend fifteen dollars instead of three on a bottle of Italian wine.

We teach our children about Italy, how to shout "*jesciallà!* go away!" in Neapolitan dialect as they chase seagulls from our picnics. They are fascinated and terrified by books about Pompeii; they eat olives and octopus, and ask questions like "Can we go to Italy for the weekend?"

Gino and I dream of the wonderful times to which we can never return. Gino's parents have passed on, Adamo too, and Tigrotto, who lived for several happy years with my parents. Ciro and Arianna have a child now, but they are separated, living on different sides of the Mediterranean, a terrible split full of anger and regret. Our Italy, the one that brought us together, lives now in our hearts, journals, and photo albums.

But we dream also of our future Italy—the one where we will spend family vacations and perhaps retire someday. We see a sunbaked villa in Sardinia or on the Amalfi coast. We smell orange blossoms and hear gentle waves upon the pebbled beach. In some dreams, our young children are there, playing like dolphins in the sea. In others, there is just a couple, perhaps a grey-haired couple, holding hands on a stone terrace as the sun sinks into the Mediterranean.

Acknowledgements

My thanks go to Gino, without whom there would have been no love, no story. To my sons, who now embody the love that lies within these pages. To the members of the Warkworth Writers' Group, who listened to endless excerpts from this book. And to my parents for reasons too innumerable to mention, but mostly for their unconditional love, which is, after all, what it's all about.

About the Author

Sheila Wright won the 2006 *Accenti* magazine award for her story "The Nature of Italy", which is an adapted excerpt from this book. "The Nature of Italy" also appeared in *Travelers' Tales: 30 Days in Italy*.

She teaches French and English and is the facilitator of the Warkworth Writers' Group.

She lives in Ontario, Canada, with her husband and two sons.

CPSIA information can be obtained at www.ICGtesting.com
Printed in the USA
237384LV00003B/56/P